Devotion

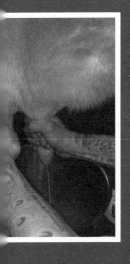

A Selection of
Raja Bhoga Recipes

Dhama Sevana Dasa

A Selection of Raja Bhoga Recipes
A Spiritual Cookbook

Dhama Sevana Dasa
Diploma in Building and Engineering, Food and Safety Level 1 and 2, Supervising Food Safety Level 3,
Cooking for the Deities since 1996

Krishna Kishor Dasa (compiler)
BSc (Hons) in Applied Chemistry, Diploma in Marketing, Supervising Food Safety Level 3,
Cooking for Deities since 2010

First Printing 2012 UK Paperback ISBN 978-0-9573008-0-4
Second Printing 2013 Revised Edition Hard Bound

Cover and interior design by Prasannatma Dasa & Yogendra Sahu
Printed in India
Published simultaneously in the United States and Canada by
Torchlight Publishing, Inc.

Library of Congress Cataloging-in-Publication Data

Dasa, Dhama Sevana, 1973-
  A selection of raja bhoga recipes / Dhama Sevana Dasa.
    pages cm
  "A spiritual cookbook."
  ISBN 978-1-937731-10-6
1. Cooking, Indic. I. Title.
  TX724.5.I4D357 2013
  641.5954--dc23
                              2013005081

For more information, contact the Publisher:

Torchlight Publishing, Inc.
PO Box 52 Badger, CA 93603
Email: torchlightpublishing@yahoo.com
Web: www.Torchlight.com

For more information about the content, contact the author:
Dhama Sevana Dasa,
Bhaktivedanta Manor, Hilfield Lane, Aldenham, Hertfordshire, WD25 8EZ, UK
www.rajabhoga.com

This cookbook is dedicated to

His Divine Grace A.C. Bhaktivedanta Swami Srila Prabhupada
and our beloved spiritual masters
His Holiness Radhanath Swami Maharaj
His Grace Krishna Kshetra Prabhu &
His Grace Jiva Pati Prabhu

CONTENTS

An Appreciation

From the day Srila Prabhupada incorporated the ISKCON movement, the preparation and offerings of food to Lord Krishna has been a devotional focal point. After establishing the first ISKCON temple at 26 second Avenue, New York, Srila Prabhupada would daily shop for vegetables, personally prepare the various dishes, lovingly offer them to the Lord, and then serve out the prasadam to his hippie guests. And, in case anyone who got hungry afterwards, Srila Prabhupada would keep a jar of gulab jamuns available at all times. He called them "ISKCON bullets"! These offerings please Lord Krishna and transform our lives.

Vaisnava culture proclaims the preparation, offering and 'honouring' of foodstuffs to be an extremely sacred activity when conducted with due care, attention and spiritual consciousness. If we place an iron rod in a fire, soon the rod becomes red hot and acts just like fire. In the same way, food prepared for and offered to Lord Krishna with love and devotion becomes completely spiritualised. Such food is called Krishna prasadam, which means "the mercy of Lord Krishna" and relishing these devotional offerings is a fundamental practice of bhakti-yoga.

Srila Prabhupada personally trained his disciples in the authentic and traditional art of cooking. He taught them everything from strict rules of cleanliness, to the appropriate use of various ingredients. He repeatedly requested that this art of cooking be preserved and developed in the ISKCON society.

This cookbook has been brought to life by two of the personal cooks of Sri Sri Radha-Gokulananda. For many years, there was a folder containing hundreds of recipes in one of the drawers in the Deity kitchen of Bhaktivedanta Manor. The folder had shown the wear and tear from years of usage-spillage, burn marks and ingredient stains marked every other page! Finally, the authors decided to fulfill their long awaited dream. Thus, this cookbook was produced out of their dedication, passion and unwavering enthusiasm to prepare the finest dishes for the pleasure of Sri Sri Radha-Gokulananda. It is a celebration of exquisite foods that have been tried and tested over many years and lovingly offered to Their Lordships.

The authors have selected well over 108 of prominent recipes that are regularly cooked for

Sri Sri Radha-Gokulananda. Although these are only a small sample of the numerous and wonderful foods that are offered daily, they illustrate the intricate art of cooking for the Lord. I think that both authors can be confident that there will be many grateful readers who will gain knowledge, skill and insight into the ancient and authentic art of cooking.

aiche anna ye krsnake karaya bhojana
janme janme sire dharon tanhara carana
(CC Madhya 3.65)

Sri Caitanya Mahaprabhu approved of all the methods employed in cooking and offering food to Krishna. Indeed, He was so pleased that He said, "Frankly, I will personally take the lotus feet of anyone who can offer Krishna such nice food and place those lotus feet on My head birth after birth".

Our very best wishes to the authors, Dhama Sevana Prabhu and Krishna Kishor Prabhu for their patience, hard work and devotion in putting this invaluable work together. It is a very special offering as we begin the preparations to celebrate the 40th anniversary of the installation of Sri Sri Radha-Gokulananda in 2013.

Your servant and well wisher

Srutidharma Dasa

Temple President

Bhaktivedanta Manor

FOREWORD

Like so many newcomers to "Krishna consciousness," my initial attraction to this unfamiliar way of life was largely through the tongue. The handfull of fruit salad I received on Telegraph Avenue in Berkeley in 1969 was the smiling monk assured me"Krishna prasadam - the mercy of God." It wasn't until the summer of 1972, in Hamburg, Germany, that I gained a deeper sense of what prasadam is: Here was my first encounter with a "real" temple (a converted warehouse upper floor) wherein charming Radha-Krishna and Jagannath deities were attended by a small crew of dedicated brahmacharis. At that time, when I peeked into the kitchen shortly before a noontime lunch offering was being prepared for the deities, I was struck by the hushed air of concentration that made me wonder if someone was undergoing a critical medical operation. For what I had begun to witness was what I would gradually appreciate much more fully: Krishna-bhakti – devotion to the supreme Lord in his charming and sublime form as the "All-Attractive One" revolves very much around the careful preparation and offering of (strictly vegetarian) food to the Lord in his physical form (murti or "Deity").

In the summer of 1973 I was fortunate to be present in Bhaktivedanta Manor when Srila Prabhupada, my spiritual master and the Founder-Acharya of ISKCON (International Society for Krishna Consciousness), came to visit this recently acquired grand residence for the deities Sri Sri Radha-Gokulananda and for a substantial number of devotees. Prabhupada wanted to see to it that the daily worship of Radha and Krishna in these beautiful marble forms would be conducted properly – with due reverence, care, devotion and lifestyle purity – following standards prescribed in ancient scriptures. Integral to the deities' daily worship would be the preparation of several food offerings, beginning with an offering of milk sweets immediately before the 4:30 a.m. mangala arati ceremony and ending with an offering of snacks and milk prior to the deities' rest for the night.

Considering the several challenges that the Bhaktivedanta Manor community has faced over the years, it is a truly astonishing fact that this very high standard of worship established by Srila Prabhupada so many decades ago has been carefully maintained and even increased, with not a single day of service missed. And the hidden centre of this attentive worship has always been the kitchen, where exclusively those devotees are permitted to cook who have received brahmana initiation (with gayatri mantra and other Pancaratrika mantras), strictly observing four "regulative principles" (not eating meat, fish or eggs; not gambling; not taking any intoxicants; and not engaging in improper sexual activity) and keeping a daily regimen of meditative chanting of the "mahamantra" – Hare Krishna Hare Krishna Krishna Krishna Hare Hare, Hare Rama Hare Rama Rama Rama Hare Hare.

Srila Prabhupada frequently expressed concern that the temple worship he had established would continue and thrive in his absence and this concern has been imbibed and developed into great resolve by his followers, already including those in the second and third generation. This book is one very practical expression of and application of such concern and resolve. Dhama Sevana Dasa, an experienced cook who shares deity kitchen managerial responsibilities with Gadadhara prabhu (head pujari) and Krishna Kishor Dasa who recently joined the deity department, are among the second generation of devotees Srila Prabhupada intended to continue with high quality deity worship. This book represents their combined years of devoted practice and experience serving Sri Sri Radha-Gokulananda through the culinary arts.

Initially intended to be an in-house user manual for novice deity cooks, happily in this nicely printed edition our authors are sharing their seasoned expertise with the wider world of Krishna-devotees. Upon initially encountering this cookbook one might think, "Surely we already have enough Krishna consciousness cookbooks available; what need is there for yet another cookbook?" However, it is clear that our authors, having imbibed the knowledge of other such cookbooks, have done rightly to communicate their well-refined sense of how preparing devotional food offerings for a particular form of Krishna can be done expertly and efficiently, in ways that are surely pleasing to the Lord (as can be experienced by honouring the Lord's prasadam). The guidance provided by this book assures that an important western Krishna temple's tradition of fine cooking for Krishna will continue and also that many Vaisnavas worldwide will have the benefit of this tradition for their own devotional practice in temple kitchens as well as home kitchens. The book also serves as an important document recording a significant aspect of Bhaktivedanta Manor's already rich history.

Whenever I have opportunity to visit Bhaktivedanta Manor in recent years, like so many thousands of visitors I look forward to having darsana of the deities, tasting their caranamrta (the mixture of water, yogurt and scents with which the deities have been bathed that morning) and tasting remnants (prasadam) of their food offerings (especially from the milk sweets, famous throughout the world, as prepared by Mother Kulangana, prepared with milk from the Manor's own cows). May all Krishna-bhaktas get such opportunity to come to Bhaktivedanta Manor and may all readers/users of this book become inspired and ever more skilled in the devotional preparation of food offerings pleasing to the Lord!

Krishna Kshetra Dasa

Oxford Centre for Hindu Studies

PREFACE

For thirty years I worked as a medicinal chemist in an organic laboratory synthesising "new chemical entities" also known as new medicines, for one of the largest pharmaceutical companies in the world. Due to reorganisations within the company an opportunity for early retirement became available to me.

My interest in Krishna Consciousness developed mainly by reading Srila Prabhupada's books. I realised that serving the Deities and Vaisnavas is key to a successful spiritual life. During 2004-2005 on Friday evenings I served maha-prasadam after the 7 pm arati for almost a year. After this period I was asked to carry out the Friday evening 7 and 9 pm transfers in the pujari room. It was during this time I met Dhama Sevana Prabhu.

I was offered early retirement in November 2008 and from January 2009 I volunteered to spend two extra days a week helping Dhama Sevana Prabhu in the Deity kitchen. While serving together in the Deity kitchen we decided through the mercy of Guru and Krishna to write this publication, which started off initially, as an aid for present and future Deity cooks to help them with preparing raja bhoga offerings for the Lordships. We are now publishing these recipes as a cookbook for anyone interested in preparing high standard quality vegetarian dishes.

The selection of recipes shown in this cookbook have been used by Dhama Sevana Prabhu for the last 15 years and he is now sharing them with us. Thank you Dhama.

Hare Krishna

Krishna Kishor Dasa

Bhaktivedanta Manor

ACKNOWLEDGEMENTS

My service to the Deities is intimate and is a privilege to undertake. I always try to maintain a good attitude of love, devotion and spirituality.

On the basis of this theme I wish to offer my sincere thanks to the following devotees:

Isa Avatara Prabhu whose recipes I used exclusively in the beginning of my cooking service.

Gadadhara Prabhu for encouraging me always to maintain a high standard not only in cooking but preparation and cleaning.

My wonderful wife Gopa Kishori Devi Dasi for her support in my spiritual life, for giving me new ideas and in some cases recipes to help improve my style of cooking.

There are also many experienced devotee cooks whom I wish to thank, Bala Gopala Devi Dasi, Kulangana Devi Dasi, Syamasundari Devi Dasi, Krishangi Devi Dasi, Vrajabhumi Devi Dasi, Guru Seva Devi Dasi, Vasanti Devi Dasi, Lalita Sakhi Devi Dasi, Sachimata Devi Dasi, Rajeshvari Devi Dasi, Mangala Charan Devi Dasi, Vraja Dhamananda Dasa, Anita Solanki and many many more devotees and friends who have given me tips during my learning process. A big thank you to all of them.

My final thanks goes to Krishna Kishor Dasa, for recording the recipes on a portable tape recorder, typing the recipes on a computer and presenting it in a form which can be followed. Thanks to his wife Lynn for editing and typing, Amanda Messer and Dorota Wojciechowska for proof reading.

Hare Krishna

Dhama Sevana Dasa

Bhaktivedanta Manor

INTRODUCTION

During a conversation between His Divine Grace Srila Prabhupada and Jamuna Devi Dasi, Srila Prabhupada, said "Cooking is a spiritual experience for Vaisnavas similar to meditation, a means of expressing love and devotion to Lord Shree Krishna".

Over fifteen years ago in 1996 Gadadhara Prabhu our head pujari asked me to cook one of the offerings for the deities. The thought petrified me as I had very little experience in cooking. I was handed a recipe for a sabji regularly prepared for the nine o'clock offering. Gadadhara Prabhu tasted it after the offering, commented that it was fine and encouraged me to cook for both the seven and nine o'clock evening offerings. Once again, I was concerned at this prospect as the seven o'clock offering involved more preparations than the nine o'clock one. Being Polish I had never cooked rice before and the thought was daunting.

In 1996 the Deity kitchen was in the outer building and I was fortunate enough to have had the help of a lady devotee who could sense my anxiety and guided me in cooking rice and halva preparations. As before I coped with this and Gadadhara Prabhu tasted the offered prasadam and complimented it. From that day onwards due to my desire to serve and please Sri Sri Radha-Gokulananda I cooked the seven and nine o'clock offerings for ten years. A natural progression to raja bhoga cooking occurred.

Raja bhoga is a more complicated endeavour. I came across vegetables unheard of in Poland e.g. karela, bhindi, parwar and dudhi. Everything was a new experience including the variety of spices. My main desire was to please to do my best and try to aim for perfection.

The greatest input into my cooking experience came from a devotee called Isa Avatara Prabhu who was cooking here at the Manor for Sri Sri Radha-Gokulananda. I rigidly followed his recipes avoiding speculation and experimentation and this approach has helped me maintain a high standard. To date these recipes have been used here at the Manor for a total of over 30 years.

It is satisfying to know that when other devotees follow these recipes the same standard is maintained.

As previously mentioned cooking is a meditation and allows creativity. It is an art through presentation and colour, e.g. yellow rice, green chutney, colourful sabjis and fruits which are pleasing to the eyes of Lord Krishna.

Cleanliness is also very important during cooking and the general rules for cleanliness are as set by Srila Prabupada and should be maintained.

The purpose of this book is to ensure that devotees in the future have access to this selection of raja bhoga recipes. We are trying to standardise the offerings in our temple and in the future this book will be incorporated into a much larger cookbook planned for the Manor which will also include recipes from other experienced devotee cooks.

Srila Bhaktivinoda Thakura has written a beautiful prayer called the Bhoga Arati (from Gitavali) made up of seventeen verses which can be sung while Krishna is partaking in the prepartions.

I would like to draw your attention to two of my favourite verses:

sukta-sakadi bhaji nalita kusmanda
dali dalna dugdha-tumbi dadhi moca-khanda

They are then served a feast of sukta and various kinds of green leafy vegetables, then nice fried things and a salad made of the green leaves of the jute plant. They are also served pumpkin, baskets, of fruit, square cakes made of lentils and cooked-down milk, then thick yogurt, squash cooked in milk and vegetables preparations made from the flower of banana tree.

mugda-bora masa-bora rotika ghrtanna
saskuli pistaka khir puli payasanna

Then they receive fried squares of mung dal patties and urad dal patties, chapatis and rice with ghee. Next sweets made with milk sugar and sesamum; rice flour cakes; thick cooked-down milk; cakes floating in milk and sweet rice.

Thank you

I remain you humble servant

Dhama Sevana Dasa

CONVERSION TABLES & COMPILER'S NOTES

Grams (gms) to Ounces (oz)	
10 g	0.35 oz
100 g	3.53 oz
200 g	7.05 oz
300 g	10.58 oz
400 g	14.11 oz
500 g	17.64 oz
600 g	21.16 oz
700 g	24.69 oz
800 g	28.22 oz
900 g	31.75 oz
1000 g (1kg)	35.27 oz

Temperature conversion		
Centigrade	Fahrenheit	Gas mark
140°C	275°F	1
150°C	300°F	2
160°C	325°F	3
180°C	350°F	4
190°C	375°F	5
200°C	400°F	6
220°C	425°F	7
230°C	450°F	8
240°C	475°F	9

Utensil Conversion	
1 tsp	5 ml
1 tbs	15 ml
1 cup	250 ml
1 pint	568 ml
1 ladle	45 ml

Centimetre conversion	
1 cm	0.39 inch
2.54 cm	1 inch
30.48 cm	1 ft

Liquid conversion		
1 USA gallon is	1 UK gallon is	1 litre
0.83 UK gallon	1.2 USA gallon	0.26 USA gallon
3.78 litres	4.54 litres	0.22 UK gallon

Useful Calculations
1000 grams is also 1 kilogram (1 kg)
1 kilogram is 2.2 lbs which is approximately 2lbs 3 ozs
Half of 1 kg is 500 grams which is approximately 18 ozs
Quarter of 1 kg is 250 grams which is approximately 9 ozs

This publication originally written for Bhaktivedanta Manor Deity cooks can also be used for home offerings. **Each recipe is enough for 8 to 10 persons**.

To prepare paneer from full fat milk (1 litre) use bottled lemon juice (approximately 85 ml).

Ghee is used for cooking and frying as the prepared food is made as an offering to the Deities and then later the sanctified food is eaten as prasadam.

Ayurveda considers ghee to be sattvik (in the mode of goodness) when used in cooking.

For home cooking you can replace ghee with olive oil and for deep-frying you can use sunflower oil.

In the Deity kitchen at Bhaktivedanta Manor the cooks almost always use goshalla milk for sweets, paneer and sweet rice preparations. We recommend you use organic full fat milk which will give a quality of paneer similar to that obtained from goshalla milk.

All offerings are decorated with Tulasi leaves which is very pleasing to Lord Krishna.

All photographys shown in this book were taken minutes before the offering. Action photos and hence not staged.

RICE

1.1 Plain rice

Ingredients

45 ml ghee

1 ½ cup basmati rice

3 ⅓ cup water

1 tsp salt

Preparation Method

In a small pot heat water (3 ⅓ cups) over a high flame.

Take basmati rice (1 ½ cups) wash it through a sieve and allow the water to drain.

To another medium sized pot add ghee (1 small ladle 45 ml) and heat over a medium to high flame.

Add the washed basmati rice (1 ½ cups) to the hot ghee and stir for about 2 minutes. When all the rice grains are completely covered with ghee add the hot water from the small pot and salt (1 tsp), cover with a lid and cook over a low flame for 10-15 minutes. Do not disturb the cooking process.

It might appear odd to use two pots for cooking rice however, using two pots gives perfectly cooked rice.

Check the rice is cooked by inserting a knife into the middle of the rice pot.

If the knife is dry when you remove it from the pot the rice is cooked, or take one grain of rice from the pot, squeeze the grain between the fingers and if that grain is soft (transparent, not white in the middle) the rice is ready to be served.

Preparation time: 5 min   Cooking time: 15 min

1.2 FANCY RICE

Ingredients

1 cup basmati rice
2 ¼ cups water
1 small chopped red pepper
hand full cashew nuts

45 ml ghee
1 tsp salt
¾ tsp tumeric
¼ tsp black pepper
½ cup frozen peas
curry leaves approx 10

Preparation Method

Fancy rice is also prepared using 2 pots.

Take medium sized red pepper (1) and dice into small pieces.

In a small pot heat water (2 ¼ cups) over a high flame.

Take basmati rice (1 cup) and wash it through a sieve and allow the water to drain.

Add ghee (1 small ladle 45 ml) to another medium sized saucepan and heat over a medium to high flame.

To the heated ghee add the finely chopped red pepper, cashew nuts (handful), some curry leaves (approximately 10). Stir for 1-2 minutes, this roasting period will allow the cashew nuts to brown and the red peppers to soften.

From the sieve add the washed rice and stir for another 1-2 minutes. Pour in the hot water from the small pot, followed by frozen peas (½ cup), salt (1 tsp), turmeric (¾ tsp), and finally black pepper (¼ tsp). Cover and cook over a low flame for 15 minutes. Do not disturb the cooking process.

Check the rice is cooked (see plain rice recipe) and serve.

Preparation time: 5 min   Cooking time: 15 min

N.B. Other variations of fancy rice are available on the next page.

1). Rice with yogurt:
Cook rice (1 cup) in ghee (45 ml) with mustard seeds (1 tsp), turmeric (½ tsp), salt (1 tsp) and boiling water (2 ¼ cups).

After the rice has cooked add yogurt (¾ cup) mix in with the rice and serve.

2). Rice with lemon:
Cook rice (1 cup) in ghee (45 ml) with turmeric (½ tsp), salt (1 tsp), ½ lemon rind and boiling water (2 ¼ cup).

After the rice has cooked add lemon juice from half a lemon, mix and serve.

3). Rice with spinach:
First wash then blend spinach (1 bunch) in a food processor. Cook rice (1 cup) in ghee (45 ml) with fenugreek (½ tsp). Next add the blended spinach followed by turmeric (½ tsp), salt (1 tsp) and hot water (2 ¼ cups). Serve when the rice is soft.

4). Rice with Spanish saffron:
Cook rice (1 cup) in ghee (45 ml), with mustard seeds (½ tsp), cumin seeds (1 tsp), Spanish saffron (½ tsp), cloves (6), a finely chopped tomato and boiling water (2 ¼ cups).

Serve when the rice is soft.

Average preparation time: 5 min   Cooking time: 15 min

DALS

Ingredients

1 cup green lentils
6-8 cups water

45 ml ghee
1 tsp mustard seeds
2 cinnamon sticks
8 dry curry leaves or
4 fresh curry leaves or
1-2 bay leaves
1 tsp fenugreek
1 tsp cumin seeds
1 tsp asafetida
2 tbs grated ginger
2 chopped chillies
1 tsp salt
fresh coriander leaves
2 blended tomatoes or
¾ cup of plain yogurt

Preparation Method

To a medium sized saucepan add green lentils (1 cup). Wash and drain. Add water (8 cups) to the washed lentils and bring to the boil over a medium flame without a lid for approximately 25 minutes or until the dal softens.

Remove the froth formed with a slotted spoon and discard.

At the end of 25 minutes the chaunce (fried seasoning and spices), is prepared by taking either the largest ladle available and add ghee (45 ml) to it or add ghee to a small pot and heat over a medium flame.

Next add mustard seeds (1 tsp), allow the seeds to pop then add cinnamon sticks (2), dry curry leaves (8) or fresh curry leaves (4) or bay leaves (1-2) fenugreek (1 tsp), cumin seeds (1 tsp), asafetida (1 tsp), grated ginger (2 tbs), chopped chillies (2).

Cook for one minute. Pour this hot sizzling mixture to the cooked lentils. Take care during the addition, as splashing occurs when hot ghee comes into contact with watery dal.

Next add salt (1 tsp) and either blended tomatoes (2) or plain yogurt (¾ cup). Cook for 5 minutes. Mix and sprinkle with washed, finely chopped fresh coriander leaves and serve with plain or fancy rice.

Preparation time: 5 min   Cooking time: 30 min

Mung dal with yogurt

Ingredients

1 cup yellow split dal
8 cups water

45 ml ghee
2 tsp cumin seeds
2 tsp whole dhania seeds
2 tbs grated ginger
2 chopped green chillies
½ tsp asafetida
1 tsp turmeric
3 blended or cut tomatoes
1 tsp salt
fresh coriander leaves

Preparation Method

To a medium sized saucepan add yellow split dal (1 cup). Wash and drain. Add water (8 cups) to the washed dal and boil over a medium flame without a lid for 20 minutes or until the dal softens.

Remove froth formed with a slotted spoon and discard.

After 20 minutes prepare the chaunce (fried seasoning and spices) in either a small saucepan or the largest stainless steel ladle.

Add ghee (45 ml) to the largest available ladle followed by cumin seeds (2 tsp), whole dhania seeds (2 tsp), chopped green chillies (2), grated ginger (2 tbs), asafetida (½ tsp) and turmeric (1 tsp).

Heat mixture for 1 minute over a medium flame and when sizzling pour the mixture into the cooked dal. Take care as splashing occurs between the hot spiced ghee and watery dal.

To complete the preparation add blended or cut tomatoes (3) and salt (1 tsp), stir and heat for a further 5 minutes. Garnish with fresh washed finely chopped coriander leaves. Serve with plain or fancy rice.

Preparation time: 5 min   Cooking time: 20 min

Ingredients

1 cup chana dal
8 cups water
½ tsp salt
2 tsp oil

45 ml ghee
1 tsp mustard seeds
1 cinnamon stick
1 tsp fenugreek
1 tsp cumin seeds
4 whole cloves
2 tbs grated ginger
2 chopped green chillies
½ tsp asafetida
3 blended tomatoes
1 tsp turmeric
1 tsp salt
fresh coriander leaves

Preparation Method

To a medium sized saucepan add chana dal (1 cup). Wash and drain.

Add water (8 cups) to the washed chana dal followed by salt (½ tsp) and oil (2 tsp). Place over a medium flame and bring to the boil for 30 minutes. Cover with a lid as chana dal takes longer to cook compared to yellow split dal or green lentil dal.

Remove froth formed with a slotted spoon and discard.

In another smaller saucepan the chaunce (fried seasoning and spices) is prepared by adding ghee (45 ml), followed by mustard seeds (1 tsp) and allow them to pop.

Next add cinnamon stick (1), fenugreek (1 tsp), cumin seeds (1 tsp), whole cloves (4-5), grated ginger (2 tbs), finely chopped green chillies (2), asafetida (½ tsp), blended tomatoes (3), followed by turmeric (1 tsp) and finally salt (1 tsp). Stir and cook for 5 minutes.

After boiling the dal for 30 minutes blend with a stick blender and add the sizzling sauce to the cooked dal. Take care as splashing occurs between the sauce and watery dal.

Mix and heat with a wooden spoon for 1-2 minutes over a medium flame. Garnish with fresh, washed and finely chopped coriander leaves. Serve with plain or fancy rice.

Preparation time: 5 min   Cooking time: 30 min

2.4 Toovar dal

Ingredients

1 cup toovar dal
8 cups water
3-4 blended tomatoes

45 ml ghee
1 tsp mustard seeds
1 cinnamon stick
3 whole cloves
2-3 bay leaves
2 tbs grated ginger
2 chopped green chillies
½ tsp asafetida
1 tsp turmeric
1 tsp salt
fresh coriander leaves

Preparation Method

To a medium sized saucepan add toovar dal (1 cup). Wash and drain.

Add water (8 cups) to the washed dal and bring to the boil over a medium flame without a lid for 20 minutes or until the dal softens.

Remove froth formed with a slotted spoon and discard.

Over a medium flame in either a small saucepan or the largest available ladle, the chaunce (fried seasoning and spices) is prepared by adding ghee (45 ml) followed by mustard seeds (1 tsp).

After the mustard seeds have popped add cinnamon stick (1), whole cloves (3), bay leaves (2-3), grated ginger (2 tbs), chopped green chillies (2), asafetida (½ tsp) and turmeric (1 tsp). Cook for 1 minute.

Pour the chaunce into the cooked dal. Take care as splashing takes occurs when the sauce is added to the watery dal.

To complete the preparation, add blended or cut tomatoes (3) and salt (1 tsp). Stir and heat for a further 5 minutes, garnish with fresh, washed and finely chopped coriander leaves and serve with plain or fancy rice.

Preparation time: 5 min   Cooking time: 20 min

Ingredients

¼ cup split mung dal
¼ cup urad dal
¼ cup chana dal
½ cup toovar dal
8 cups water
½ tsp salt

45 ml ghee
1 tsp cumin seeds
½ tsp whole dhania seeds
3 red chillies
1 cinnamon stick
1 tbs grated ginger
½ tsp asafetida
1 tsp turmeric
8 curry leaves
3 blended tomatoes
1 tsp salt
½ bunch fresh coriander

Preparation Method

Mix split mung dal (¼ cup), urad dal (¼ cup), chana dal (¼ cup) and toovar dal (½ cup) in a medium sized saucepan. Wash and drain.

Add water (8 cups) and salt (½ tsp) and bring to the boil over a medium flame until the chana dal softens.

Remove froth formed with a slotted spoon and discard.

Over a medium flame in a small saucepan the chaunce (fried seasoning and spices) is prepared with ghee (45 ml) and cumin seeds (1 tsp).

Allow the cumin seeds to sizzle then add whole dhania seeds (½ tsp), red chillies (3), cinnamon stick (1), grated fresh ginger (1 tbs), asafetida (½ tsp), turmeric (1 tsp), curry leaves (8) and blended tomatoes (3).

Cook for 5 minutes over a medium flame then pour the prepared sauce into the cooked dal. Add salt (1 tsp) mix thoroughly. Garnish with washed and finely chopped coriander leaves, and serve with plain or fancy rice.

Preparation time: 5 min   Cooking time: 20 min

2.6 KADEE SAUCE

Ingredients

3 cups yogurt
3 cups water
⅓ cup chickpea flour
2 tsp salt
2 green chillies
1 tbs grated fresh ginger
3 tbs grated jaggery
1 tsp turmeric

45 ml ghee
3 cinnamon sticks
4 cloves, whole
1 tsp cumin seeds
1 tsp asafetida
8-10 dry curry leaves

Preparation Method

In either a mixing jug or a medium sized saucepan add yogurt (3 cups), water (3 cups), chickpea flour (⅓ cup), salt (2 tsp), finely chopped green chillies (2), grated fresh ginger (1 tbs), grated or crushed jaggery (3 tbs) and turmeric (1 tsp).

Whisk to a smooth texture and set aside.

In a medium sized saucepan a mixture of spices (chaunce) is prepared in ghee (45 ml) with cinnamon sticks (3), whole cloves (4), cumin seeds (1 tsp), asafetida (1 tsp) and dry curry leaves (8-10). Stir and cook for 1-2 minutes over a medium flame.

Add the whisked yogurt mixture to the spiced mixture (chaunce). Bring to the boil over a high flame. Adjust the flame to medium-low. Allow to cook for 15 minutes with occasional stirring. The kadee sauce is ready for serving with plain rice.

Preparation time: 5 min   Cooking time: 20 min

WET SABJIS

3.1 Potatoes Cauliflower and Peas

Ingredients

1 medium sized cauliflower (800 g)
5 medium sized potatoes
½ cup frozen peas
4-5 medium sized tomatoes

65 ml ghee
1 tsp mustard seeds
1 tsp cumin seeds
2 tsp whole coriander seeds
½ tsp asafetida
2 chopped green chillies
2 tbs grated ginger
1 ½ tsp salt
1-1½ tsp sugar
½ tsp garam masala
1 tsp turmeric
2 tsp lemon juice
½ bunch fresh coriander leaves

Preparation Method

Trim one medium sized cauliflower and cut into florets (4 cm) long and (2.5 cm) thick. Rinse in a colander and allow to drain. Potatoes (5) are washed peeled and cut into medium sized cubes and set aside in a colander. Frozen peas (½ cup) added to a sieve and washed in hot water.

In a saucepan large enough to cook all the vegetables over a medium flame, add ghee (1-1½ ladle 65 ml), followed by mustard seeds (1 tsp) and allow them to pop.

Next add cumin seeds (1 tsp), allow them to sizzle, then add whole coriander seeds (1 tsp), asafetida (½ tsp), finally chopped green chillies (2) and grated ginger (2 tbs).

Stir the first set of spices for about 1-2 minutes with a wooden spoon allowing the ingredients to cook. Add the prepared vegetables and mix now add the second set of spices, salt (1 ½ tsp), sugar (1 ½ tsp), garam masala (½ tsp) and turmeric (1 tsp).

Mix the contents of the pot again with a wooden spoon cover and cook for 15 minutes on a medium flame. Water (½ cup) can be added to prevent sticking and burning. When the vegetables are almost cooked add blended tomatoes (4-5) and cook for a further 5 minutes. Add lemon juice (2 tsp) and garnish with washed, finely chopped fresh coriander leaves and serve.

Preparation time: 15 min   Cooking time: 20 min

Ingredients

1.2 kg (7-8 bunches of spinach)
3 litres full fat milk
250 ml bottled lemon juice
½ cup water

1 ½ ladle ghee 65 ml
1 tsp mustard seeds
1 tsp fenugreek seeds
1 bay leaf
2 chopped green chillies
2 tbs grated ginger
½ tsp asafetida
1 tsp turmeric
1 ½ tsp salt

Preparation Method

Paneer preparation: (Boiling time 30 min, filtering and pressing time 10-30 min)

Paneer or home made cheese is made by boiling full fat milk (3 litres) over a medium flame in a pot large enough to allow the milk to rise without overflowing.

When the milk begins to rise remove from the heat, stir in the curdling agent which could be either bottled lemon juice (1 cup, 250 ml), citric acid (2 tsp) or yogurt (1 cup, 250 ml). In this example bottled lemon juice was used as the curdling agent. When the milk has boiled remove the pot from the heat add the bottled lemon juice (250 ml) and almost immediately sponge like paneer separates from the yellow-green whey. If the whey is not clear add a further amount of lemon juice and stir again.

After the curd has separated out completely collect the curd in a cheese cloth covering a large colander. Rinse the collected curd under a cold tap for half a minute to make the curd firm and free from lemon juice. Twist the cheese cloth and place a cooking pot filled with water on top of the twisted cheese cloth to remove all the liquid which will run out in all directions. Leave the paneer under this heavy weight between 10 minutes to 30 minutes.

Take spinach (7-8 bunches, 1.2 kg), cut into medium sized pieces on a chopping board and place into a large bowl or kitchen sink filled with lukewarm water. These cut pieces are now agitated by hand to ensure all the spinach is free of sand. The spinach is removed from the sink using flat topped colanders (2), excess water drains out and the filled colanders are set aside.

Remove the pot full of water sitting on top of the paneer unwind the twisted cheese cloth leaving dry and flattened paneer. Cut into medium sized cubes and set aside.

In a large tall pot over a medium flame, add ghee (1-1½ ladle 65 ml) followed by (1 tsp) mustard seeds. When the mustard seeds have popped add bay leaf (1) then fenugreek seeds (1 tsp), followed by asafetida (½ tsp), chopped green chillies (2) and grated ginger (2 tbs). Rapidly add the washed spinach (2 colanders), followed by salt (1 tsp) and turmeric (1 tsp), stir to mix all the ingredients. Add water (½ cup), cover with a lid and allow the spinach to cook for 15 minutes. When the spinach is reduced to half its original size add the cubed paneer plus salt (½ tsp) and mix gently.

Several other options are now open to individual preferences before serving.
- Fry cubed paneer over a medium flame in a karhai / wok or a deep-frying pan until golden brown and add to the spinach at the end of the cooking.
- Add fried cubed potatoes (4 medium sized) or (½) a cubed pumpkin when the spinach is cooked instead of paneer. With the pumpkin cook until soft and then serve.
- Add cubed potatoes (4 medium sized) with the spinach at the beginning of cooking and at the end add either fried cubed paneer or cubed paneer (not fried).
- Add soured cream (1cup) stir and mix and then add the paneer or fried potatoes.
- Add cashew nuts or peas at the beginning of the cooking before the spinach is added.

Preparation time: 20 min   Cooking time: 15 min

3.3 Deep-fried aubergine red / green peppers and paneer in tomato sauce

Ingredients

2 aubergines
2-3 red / green peppers
2 litres full fat milk
125 ml bottled lemon juice
5 blended tomatoes
¼ cup raisins

65 ml ghee
1 ½ tsp whole coriander seeds
1 tsp cumin seeds
¼ tsp fenugreek seeds
2 tbs grated ginger
2 chopped green chillies
½ tsp paprika powder
½ tsp asafetida
1 ½ tsp salt
1 tsp turmeric
⅔ tsp black pepper
⅓ tsp garam masala
1 tsp sugar or jaggery
½ bunch fresh coriander

Preparation Method

Prepare the cubed paneer as described in the recipe 3.2 using full fat milk (2 litres) and bottled lemon juice (125 ml).

Wash and cut into medium sized cubes red or green peppers (2 or 3). Green peppers are preferred as they add colour to the dish. Aubergines either (3) medium or (2) large, are also washed and cut into medium sized cubes. Both vegetables are kept in separate colanders.

Line two flat topped colanders with a kitchen roll to absorb excess ghee.

Fill a karhai / wok or a deep-frying pan three quarters full with ghee and heat over a medium flame.

First fry the peppers and when soft remove with a slotted spoon drain and leave standing in the lined colander.

Next fry the cubed paneer until golden brown and treat in the same way as the peppers and stand in another lined colander.

Increase the flame to high and rapidly fry the cubed aubergines remove with a slotted spoon drain the excess ghee and add to the colander which has the paneer.

In a large saucepan over a medium flame add ghee (1-1½ small ladle 65 ml), followed by whole coriander seeds (1 ½ tsp), cumin seeds (1 tsp), fenugreek (¼ tsp), grated ginger (2 tbs), chopped green chilli (2), paprika powder (½ tsp), asafetida (½ tsp) and blended tomatoes (5).

Next add salt (1 ½ tsp), turmeric (1 tsp), black pepper (1 tsp), garam masala (⅓ tsp), sugar or jaggery (1 tsp).

Allow the mixture to cook for 5-10 minutes until the tomato juice begins to bubble. At this stage add raisins (¼ cup), the fried vegetables and paneer to the bubbling tomato mixture. Stir the sabji in the seasoned tomato sauce, sprinkle with lemon juice, garnish with washed and chopped fresh coriander and serve.

N.B. It is important to fry the aubergine rapidly at a higher temperature, this prevents them from becoming saturated with ghee.

Preparation time: 20 min   Cooking time: 25 min

3.4 DEEP-FRIED CAULIFLOWER POTATOES AND AUBERGINE

Ingredients

1 medium sized cauliflower approx 800 g
5 medium sized potatoes
1 large aubergine
1 cup soured cream

1 ½ tsp salt
¾ tsp asafetida
1 tsp turmeric
1-1 ½ tsp dhana jeera
1-1 ½ tsp black pepper

Additional vegetables
1-2 red peppers
½ -1 cup cashew nuts
¾ cup frozen peas

Preparation Method

One medium sized cauliflower is washed, cut into florets 4 cm long x 2.5 cm thick and placed in a flat topped colander.

Wash peel and cut potatoes (5) into medium sized cubes.

Next take a large aubergine remove the stem and cut into medium sized cubes.

Line a flat topped colander with kitchen roll to absorb excess ghee.

Fill a karhai / wok or deep-frying pan three quarters full with ghee an heat over a medium flame.

First fry the cauliflower florets remove with a slotted and transfer to the the lined colander.

Allow excess ghee to be absorbed onto the paper and then transfer the fried cauliflower from the colander to a stainless steel cooking pot. Next fry the cubed potatoes drain the ghee and add to the colander and then transfer to the pot. At a higher temperature fry the aubergines repeat draining ghee procedure and add to the stainless steel pot. Remember to change the used kitchen roll for the different fried vegetables.

Other vegetable mentioned peppers and cashew nuts can also be fried and included in the sabji or bring to the boil frozen peas (¾ cup) until soft then add to the fried vegetables.

The stainless steel cooking pot should now have all the fried vegetables.

Season with salt (1 ½ tsp), asafetida (¾ tsp), turmeric (1 tsp), dhana jeera (1-1 ½ tsp) and black ground pepper (1-1 ½ tsp). Add soured cream (1 cup). Mix while warming on a medium flame for 5 minutes and serve.

N.B. It is important to fry the aubergine rapidly at a higher temperature, this prevents the aubergines from becoming saturated with ghee.

Preparation time: 20 min   Frying time: 25 min

3.5 Toria

Ingredients

12-13 torias
¾ cup white poppy seeds

45 ml ghee
1 tbs cumin seeds
2 tsp grated ginger
2 chopped green chillies
1 tsp asafetida
1 ½ tsp salt
1 tsp turmeric

Preparation Method

Choose toria (12-13) larger size, are preferred. Wash and peel into strips, remembering not to peel completely. Cut into equal sized cubes and set aside in a colander.

In a coffee grinder blend poppy seeds (¾ cup) to a fine powder and set aside.

In a large pot standing over a high flame add ghee (45 ml) followed by cumin seeds (1 tbs), allow to sizzle then add the grated ginger (2 tsp), chopped green chillies (2) and asafetida (1 tsp), mix with a wooden spoon.

Next add the cubed toria followed by salt (1 ½ tsp) and turmeric (1 tsp), mix and allow to cook for 15 minutes over the high flame. There is no need to add any extra water as the torias release their own juice. Stir every 3-5 minutes to prevent them from burning.

After almost 15 minutes of cooking, the toria would have reduced to ⅓ of its original size and softened. Now add the blended white poppy seeds and mix with a stainless spoon. Lower the flame to medium and cook for 1 to 2 minutes longer. Remove from the heat and serve.

Preparation time: 10 min   Cooking time: 15 min

3.6 LAUKI / DUDHI PEAS AND PANEER IN TOMATO SAUCE

Ingredients

2 laukis / dudhis
1 cup peas
2.2 litres full fat milk
180 ml bottled lemon juice
4-6 medium sized tomatoes

65 ml ghee
1 tsp cumin seeds
½ tsp fenugreek seeds
2 chopped green chillies
2 tbs grated ginger
½ tsp asafetida
1 ½ tsp salt
½ tsp sugar
1 tsp turmeric
½ tsp garam masala
½ cup single cream
fresh coriander leaves

Preparation Method

Prepare the cubed paneer as described in recipe 3.2 with full fat milk (2.2 litres) and bottled lemon juice (180 ml).

Next wash, peel and cube laukis / dudhis (2) and set aside. Take frozen peas (1 cup) add to a sieve wash with hot water and set aside.

Add ghee (1-1 ½ small ladle 65 ml) to a large pot over a medium flame, followed by cumin seeds (1 tsp), allow to sizzle then add fenugreek seeds (½ tsp), chopped green chillies (2), grated ginger (2 tbs) and asafetida (½ tsp).

To the mixture of spices add washed, peeled and cubed pieces of lauki followed by the peas.

Add salt (1 ½ tsp), sugar (½ tsp), turmeric (1 tsp), garam masala (½ tsp) and mix. Cook for 10 minutes.

Blended tomatoes (4-6) are added to the pot followed by single cream (½ cup) and either fried cubed paneer or cubed paneer (not fried).

Stir and cook for a further 5 minutes. Garnish with washed and finely chopped fresh coriander leaves and serve.

Preparation time: 15 min   Cooking time: 20 min

Ingredients

1 cup chana dal
1 large or 2 small laukis

45 ml ghee
1 tsp mustard seeds
1 tsp asafetida
2 green chillies
2 tbs grated ginger
2 tsp salt
1 tsp turmeric
1 tbs dhana jeera
1 tbs jaggery
3-4 tomatoes
1 bunch fresh coriander leaves
2 tbs lemon juice
100 g shredded cabbage is an optional extra

Preparation Method

To a medium sized cooking pot add chana dal (1 cup). Wash several times with water, add water (4 cups) and allow to stand for one hour.

Lauki / dudhi (1 large or 2 medium sized) is washed peeled and cut into cubes and set aside in a flat topped colander.

To a large saucepan over a medium flame, the chaunce (mixture of spices) is prepared in ghee (1 small ladle 45 ml). Add mustard seeds (1 tsp) allow them to pop then add asafetida (1 tsp), chopped green chillies (2) and grated fresh ginger (1 tbs).

Pour the soaked dal into the chaunce and mix. Take care as spluttering will occur.

Continue to cook the spiced chana dal over a medium flame (15-20 minutes) or until the dal is half cooked. Test by carefully squeezing one pulse (dal) between fingers.

At this stage add the cubed lauki followed by salt (2 tsp), turmeric (1 tsp), dhana jeera (1 tsp), jaggery (1 tbs) and blended tomatoes (3-4).

Continue cooking for a further 5-10 minutes over a medium flame. Sprinkle with lemon juice (2 tbs), garnish with washed and finely chopped coriander leaves and serve.

As an option reduce the blended tomatoes down to (2) and add shredded cabbage (100 g). Cook for a further 5-10 minutes and serve.

Preparation time: 10 min   Soaking time: 60 min   Cooking time: 30 min

Ingredients

1 large or 2 medium sized laukis
1 ½ cup chickpea flour
½ cup rice flour
1 bunch fresh coriander
1 tbs lemon juice
2 chopped green chillies
2 tbs grated ginger
¾ tsp salt
1 tsp turmeric
½ tsp asafetida
1 ½ tsp coriander seed
1 tsp ENO

45 ml ghee
1 ½ tsp fenugreek seeds
½ tsp asafetida
1 chopped green chillies
1 tbs grated ginger
1 tsp salt
½ tsp turmeric
1 tsp sugar
4-5 blended tomatoes
1 cup single cream
1 bunch coriander leaves

Preparation Method

Wash, peel and grate lauki [(1 large), or (2 medium) sized] into a large mixing bowl. Add chickpea flour (1 ½ cup), rice flour (½ cup) and washed, finely chopped fresh coriander leaves (1 bunch).

Next sprinkle lemon juice (1 tbs), followed by finely chopped green chillies (2), grated ginger (2 tbs), salt (¾ tsp), turmeric (1 tsp), asafetida (½ tsp) and whole coriander seeds (1 ½ tsp). Mix, now add ENO (1 tsp), mix again to give a fairly thick batter. Most of the water comes from lauki. The mixture is ready for frying.

Line a flat topped colander with kitchen roll to absorb excess ghee.

In a karhai / wok or a deep-frying pan fill three quarters with ghee and heat over a medium flame.

Using the first three fingers and thumb of the right hand, make small balls and carefully introduce the lauki balls into the hot ghee pushing the lauki batter with the thumb.

Fry until golden brown in colour.

As batches of the lauki koftas are cooked, drain and transfer to the lined colander then set aside to cool.

In a large pot over a medium flame add ghee (1 small ladle 45 ml). Spice with fenugreek seeds (1 ½ tsp), asafetida (½ tsp), finely chopped chillies (1) and grated ginger (1 tbs).

Pour in blended tomatoes (4-5), salt (1 tsp), turmeric (½ tsp), sugar (1 tsp), followed by single cream (1 cup), continue the cooking process for 5-10 minutes.

Add the fried koftas. Mix without breaking the kofta balls, sprinkle with washed finely chopped and washed fresh coriander leaves and serve.

Preparation time: 10 min   Frying time: 20 min   Cooking time: 20 min

3.9 Smokey or burnt aubergine with peas and potatoes

Ingredients

5 aubergines
4 potatoes
1 cup frozen peas

65 ml ghee
1 ½ tsp mustard seeds
1 tsp cumin seeds
2 tbs grated ginger
2 chopped green chillies
1 tsp dhana jeera
1 ½ tsp salt
1 ½ tsp turmeric
1 tsp garam masala

Preparation Method

Wash, peel and cut potatoes (4) into small cubes and set aside in a colander.

Add frozen peas (1 cup) into a sieve wash with hot water and set aside.

Aubergines (5) are washed and placed directly on five separate flames set on high. Turn them over at regular interval with metal chapati tongs to ensure uniform cooking.

A burning smell is a good indicator of cooking. When the skin on the aurbergines begins to blister turn the flames off and remove them carefully using tongs and collect in a pot. Allow to cool to room temperature or add cold water to cool them down rapidly.

When the aubergines have cooled down, cut off the ends and discard. Peel the soft and cooled aubergines. Discard the skin and place the cooked flesh into another pot and blend to a pulp with a stick blender or cut into smaller pieces with a knife.

To a large non-stick saucepan, over a medium flame, add ghee (1-1 ½ small ladle 65 ml) and mustard seeds (1 ½ tsp), allow the seeds to pop then add cumin seeds (1 tsp), followed by grated ginger (2 tbs), finely chopped green chillis (2) and dhana jeera (1 tsp).

Add cubed potatoes to the cooking spices followed by defrosted peas (1 cup), salt (1 ½ tsp), turmeric (1 ½ tsp) and garam masala (1 tsp).

Stir and when the potatoes and peas are almost cooked, add the blended aubergines, stir for a further 5-10 minutes and serve.

N.B. To enhance the flavour and texture of this sabji add blended tomatoes (4) after the addition of the blended aubergines.

Aubergines can be oven baked for 30 minutes instead of cooking directly on the flame.

Preparation time: 15 min   Cooking time: 20 min

3.10 Sukta (Bengali dish)

Ingredients

3 karelas
1 aurbergine
3 green cooking bananas (matoki)
½ butternut squash or small ½ pumpkin
2 drumsticks
2 cups yogurt
6 cups water

45 ml ghee
1 ½ tbs punch pooran
1 tbs grated ginger
2 chopped green chillies
2-3 bay leaves
1 tsp asafetida
¾ tsp turmeric
1 ½ tsp salt
1 ½ tbs mustard powder or roasted mustard seeds

Preparation Method

It is always important to include karela in sukta preparations.
Chose medium sized karela (3) and aubergine (1) wash, top and tail cut into cubes and

set aside in two different colanders.

Take green cooking bananas also referred to as matoki (3), wash and peel while submerged in a bowl of water to prevent staining of the hands and rapid blackening of the bananas. Cut into half then into cubes and keep submerged under water.

Next either peel a washed butternut squash (½) or a small pumpkin (½) *not both*. Cut into medium sized cubes and set aside in a colander. Chose drumsticks (2) wash and with a potato peeler partially peel them and then cut into approximatley 3 cm lengths, and collect in another collander.

At this stage of the preparation there should be five prepared vegetables, cubed karela, aubergine and butternut squash or pumpkin in separate colanders. Cubed green bananas immersed under water and 3 cm lengths drumsticks in another colander.

Line 2 colanders with kitchen roll to absorb excess ghee. Fill a karhai / wok or a deep-frying pan three quarters full with ghee and heat over a medium flame.

Deep-fry the karela first remove with a slotted spoon drain excess ghee and set aside in the lined colander. Next drain away water and deep-fry the cubed green bananas until golden, remove and drain excess ghee and add to the fried karela. Over a higher flame rapidly fry the aubergine remove with a slotted spoon drain and add to a different lined colander.

In a large saucepan over a medium flame add ghee (45 ml), spoon in punch pooran (1 ½ tbs), grated ginger (1 tbs), chopped green chillies (2), bay leaves (2-3), asafetida (1 tsp). Next add yogurt (2 cups). Mix all the ingredients and cook for 1-2 minutes. Add the cut drumsticks followed by water (6 cups), mix and cook for 5 minutes.

Now add the cubed butternut squash or cubed pumpkin followed by turmeric (¾ tsp) and salt (1 ½ tsp). Continue cooking for 15 minutes until the cubed squash and drumsticks are three quarter cooked then add the fried karela and green bananas. Mix with a stainless spoon and cook for 3-5 minutes. During this time roast mustard seeds (1 ½ tbs) to popping transfer to a coffee grinder add a pinch of salt and grind to a powder. Return to the cooked vegetables add the fried aubergine immediately followed by the ground mustard seeds mix and serve. **Another option** is to add mustard powder (1 ½ tbs) instead of mustard seeds mix and serve.

N.B. As already mentioned green cooking bananas can be replaced with potatoes (1-2). Butternut squash or pumpkin can also be replaced with sweet potatoes (1-2). Drumsticks replaced with French beans (100 g) cut in half would also be acceptable.

Preparation time: 15 min   Frying time: 25 min   Cooking time: 20 min

3.11 SWEETCORN IN TOMATO JUICE AND SINGLE CREAM

Ingredients

5-6 corn on a cob
5 large tomatoes
1 cup single cream

45 ml ghee
1 ½ tsp fenugreek seeds
½ tsp asafetida
2 tbs grated ginger
2 chopped green chillies
1 ½ tsp salt
1 tbs brown sugar or jaggery
1-1 ½ tsp dhana jeera
⅓ tsp garam masala

Preparation Method

Remove the husks and threads from the sweetcorn (5-6) wash and then immerse the cobs in a pot of boiling water. Cover and over a high flame boil for approximately 10 minutes.

The sweetcorn is cooked when the corn is easily pierced with a knife.

Remove the pot from the heat, allow to cool and drain the water. Cut the cooled cobs into 2 cm rings and set aside in colander.

Clean and re-use the large pot which was used for boiling the sweetcorn.

To the pot over a medium flame, add ghee (1 small ladle 45 ml), fenugreek seeds (1 ½ tsp), asafetida (½ tsp), grated ginger (2 tbs), chopped green chillies (2) and cook for 1 minute. Add blended tomatoes (5-6) to the spices.

Next add salt (1 ½ tsp), brown sugar (1 tbs) or grated jaggery (1 tbs), dhana jeera (1-1 ½ tsp) and garam masala (⅓ tsp). Cook this tomato sauce for 10 minutes to a thick consistency similar to bottled tomato sauce.

At the end of this cooking period add single cream (1 cup), followed by the addition of the sweetcorn rings. Mix together and heat for another 5 minutes and serve.

Preparation time: 15 min   Cooking time: 35 min

3.12 Tomato peas and paneer

Ingredients

4 litres full fat milk
8 large tomatoes
½ cup frozen peas
340 ml bottled lemon juice
125 ml single cream

45 ml ghee
1 ½ tsp fenugreek seeds
2 chopped green chillies
2 tbs grated ginger
1 tsp asafetida
1 ½ tsp salt
½ tsp turmeric
½ tsp garam masala
1 tbs brown sugar or jaggery
fresh coriander leaves

Preparation Method

Prepare cubed paneer as described in recipe 3.2 using full fat milk (4 litres) and bottled lemon juice (340 ml).

Wash and blend large tomatoes (8) and set aside.

Take frozen peas (½ cup) add to a sieve wash with hot water and set aside.

To a large saucepan, over a medium flame, add ghee (45 ml), fenugreek seeds (1 ½ tsp), chopped green chillies (2), grated ginger (2 tbs), asafetida (1 tsp). Cook and stir for 1 minute. Pour in the blended tomatoes, add salt (1 ½ tsp), turmeric (½ tsp), garam masala (½ tsp) and brown sugar or jaggery (1 tbs) followed by the defrosted peas and mix.

Cover with a lid and cook for 10-15 minutes.

Add the paneer pieces (not fried) to the tomato sauce gently mix with a stainless steel spoon and cook for a further 5 minutes.

Another variation to this recipe is to fry the cubed paneer over a medium flame in a karhai / wok or deep-frying pan filled three quarters with ghee. After the cubed paneer pieces are golden brown in colour remove from the hot ghee with a slotted spoon, drain and soak in a bowl of hot water with salt (½ tsp) and turmeric (½ tsp) or immerse the fried paneer cubes in a bowl of whey for 1-2 minutes. Remove the paneer again with a slotted spoon and add to the tomato and peas sauce. Cook for a further 5 minutes.

Single cream (½ cup, 125ml) can also be added at this stage stir and heat for 1-2 minutes.

Garnish with handful of washed, chopped fresh coriander leaves and serve.

Preparation time: 20 min   Cooking time: 20 min

3.13 Aubergine potatoes and peas

Ingredients

2 medium aubergines
4 large potatoes
80 ml water
½ cup frozen peas
3 tomatoes

45 ml ghee
1 tsp mustard seeds
1 tsp asafetida
1 tsp chilli powder
1 tbs dhana jeera
1 tsp turmeric
1 ½ tsp salt
1 tbs jaggery
2 tbs lemon juice

Preparation Method

Wash and cut aubergines (2) into medium sized cubes. Choose large potatoes (4) wash, peel and cut into smaller sized cubes than the aubergine cubes. Take frozen peas (1 cup) add to a sieve wash with hot water and set aside.

To a large non stick pot over a medium flame, add ghee (1 ladle 45 ml) followed by mustard seeds (1 tsp). Allow them to pop then add asafetida (1 tsp) and stir.

Add the cubed potatoes first then water (80 ml), and cook for 5-10 minutes. Now add the cubed aubergines, frozen peas (½ cup), followed by chilli powder (1 tsp), dhana jeera (1 tbs), turmeric (1 tsp) and finally salt (1 ½ tsp).

Cook in the juices for 10 minutes. At this stage add jaggery (1 tbs) and mix.

Next add blended tomatoes (3). Cook for a further 5 minutes, sprinkle with lemon juice (2 tbs) and serve.

Preparation time: 15 min   Cooking time: 20 min

Ingredients

2 large potatoes
4 large carrots
2 peppers (yellow, red)
1 large or 2 small broccoli
700 ml yogurt

45 ml ghee
1 tsp mustard seeds
1 tsp kalonji seeds
½ tsp ginger powder
½ tsp asafetida
½ tsp paprika powder
½ tsp dhana jerra
¼ tsp black pepper
1 ½ tsp salt
1 tsp turmeric

Preparation Method

Wash all the vegetables first.

Potatoes (2) and carrots (4) are peeled and cut into chips. Set aside in separate colanders.

Chose yellow or red peppers (2), cut and remove seeds, continue cutting into strips and set aside in a different colander.

Broccoli (1 large or 2 small) are cut into small florets. Boil in a pot of water over a medium flame for 5-7 minutes. Turn off the heat drain the water and leave standing.

Line a colander with kitchen roll to absorb excess ghee.

Fill a karhai / wok or deep-frying pan three quarters full with ghee and heat over a medium flame.

First fry the chip shaped potatoes, remove with a slotted spoon and place them into the lined colander.

Next fry the chip shaped carrots, remove with the same slotted spoon, tap it on the inside of the karhai to drain the ghee and add the fried carrots to the same colander as the potatoes.

Add ghee (l ladle 45 ml) to a medium sized saucepan make the chaunce over a medium flame.

First add mustard powder (1 tsp) allow to pop, followed by kalonji seeds (1 tsp), ginger powder (½ tsp), asafetida (½ tsp) and paprika powder (½ tsp).

Introduce the peppers mix for 5 minutes then add the boiled broccoli followed by the fried potatoes and carrots.

Sprinkle salt (1 ½ tsp), turmeric (1 tsp), dhana jeera (1 tsp) and black pepper (¼ tsp).

Mix with a stainless spoon and heat for a further 2-3 minutes.

Remove from the heat, add plain yogurt (700 ml) stir and serve.

Preparation time: 20 min   Frying time: 20 min

DRY SABJIS

4.1 GREEN COOKING BANANAS (MATOKI)

Ingredients

10-12 green cooking bananas

45 ml ghee
1 tsp mustard seeds
1 tsp cumin seeds
5 fresh curry leaves or 10 dry curry leaves
2 chopped green chillies
2 tbs grated ginger
¾ tsp asafetida

Sauce
½ cup water
1 tsp turmeric
4 tsp garam masala
1 ½ tsp salt

Preparation Method

Green cooking bananas (10-12) are peeled underwater in a kitchen sink to prevent staining the hands purple. Peeling under water also prevents the bananas from going black. The peeled bananas are cut into cubes and kept underwater in a stainless steel bowl.

Ghee (1 ladle 45 ml) is added to a large non-stick cooking pot over a medium flame. Toss in mustard seeds (1 tsp) and allow them to pop.

Next add cumin seeds (1 tsp), asafetida (¾ tsp), fresh curry leaves (5), chopped green chillies (2) and crushed ginger (2 tbs).

Empty the water from the stainless steel bowl and add the cubed bananas to the pot.

Cook for 15 minutes, stir and if necessary add water (½ cup) to prevent sticking.

In a small mixing bowl make a sauce with water (½ cup), turmeric powder (1 tsp), garam masala (4 tsp) and salt (1 ½ tsp). Mix and add this sauce to the cooking bananas. Continue cooking for a further 5 minutes and serve.

N.B. To make a wet sabji follow the recipe as above. Add blended tomatoes (3) before adding the sauce, mix thoroughly. Heat for a further 5-10 on a medium flame and serve.

Preparation time: 15 min   Cooking time: 20 min

4.2 Drumsticks in White Poppy Seeds

Ingredients

15 drumsticks
2 cups water

35 ml ghee
2 chopped green chillies
2 tbs grated ginger
1 tsp asafetida
1 ½ tsp salt
1 tsp turmeric
¾ cup poppy seeds
2 tsp mustard powder (optional)

Preparation Method

Take drumsticks (15), wash and scrape gently the surfaces with a potato peeler.

Cut into 4 ½ cm lengths and place in a colander.

To a large non-stick wok add ghee (¾ ladle 35 ml) and heat over a medium flame.

Stir in chopped green chillies (2), grated ginger (2 tbs), asafetida (1 tsp) followed by the drumstick pieces.

Next add water (1 ½ cup), salt (1 ½ tsp) and turmeric (1 tsp). Stir, cover and cook for 15 minutes.

During this cooking period grind white poppy seeds (¾ cup) in a coffee grinder to a fine powder and add the ground poppy seeds to the wok.

To enhance the taste add mustard powder (2 tsp) which is an optional extra.

At the point when the drumsticks are almost cooked add water (½ cup). Heat for 5 more minutes mix and serve.

Preparation time: 10 min   Cooking time: 15-20 min

Ingredients

10 karelas
4 medium sized potatoes

2 tsp black salt
1 tbs lemon juice
1-2 crushed green chillies or
½ tsp chilli powder
2 tbs grated ginger

Preparation Method

Pick karelas (10), wash and cut into thin rings or coin shapes. Collect the rings in a large colander and set aside.

Line a colander with kitchen roll to absorb excess ghee.

Fill a karhai / wok or deep-frying pan three quarters with ghee and heat over a medium flame.

Add karela rings handful at a time, taking care not to overfill the karhai as this will cause hot ghee to spill over.

Deep-fry until crispy then remove the fried karela with a slotted spoon and transfer to the lined colander.

Tip the fried karela into a large cooking pot for seasoning. Discard the kitchen roll.

On a slightly lower flame fry the potatoes (4 medium sized) which are washed, peeled and cut into either rings or chips. Remove the potatoes after frying with a slotted spoon drain and transfer to the same pot as the karela for seasoning.

Add black salt (2 tsp) and sprinkle with either fresh lemon juice or bottled lemon juice (1 tbs).

According to individual preferences extra seasoning can be added such as crushed green chilli (2) and grated ginger (2 tbs) or chilli powder (½ tsp).

Toss the contents of the pot add to bowls and serve.

Preparation time: 15 min   Frying time: 20 min

4.4 Cooked karela

Ingredients

8-10 karelas
2-3 medium sized tomatoes

45 ml ghee
1 tsp mustard seeds
1 tsp cumin seeds
½ tsp asafetida
3 dry red chillies
2 tbs grated ginger
1 ½ tsp salt
1 tsp turmeric
¾ cup grated jaggery
fresh coriander leaves

Preparation Method

Karelas (8-10) are washed. To remove some of the bitterness, skim off the surface of the skin by scrapping gently with a potato peeler and cut into cubes. Collect in a large colander and set aside.

To large non-stick wok add ghee (1 ladle 45 ml) and heat over a medium flame.

Toss in mustard seeds (1 tsp) and allow the seeds to pop.

Next add cumin seeds (1 tsp), asafetida (½ tsp), dry red chillies (3) and grated ginger (2 tbs).

Introduce the cubed karela followed by salt (1 ½ tsp) and turmeric (1 tsp).

Allow the karela to cook for 15 minutes.

Add grated jaggery (¾ cup) mix and allow to melt, now add medium sized cubed tomatoes (3-4). Cook for a further 5 minutes.

Mix, sprinkle with freshly cut and washed coriander leaves and serve.

Preparation time: 15 min   Cooking time: 20 min

4.5 Deep-fried karela potatoes and tomatoes

Ingredients

6 karelas
2-3 medium sized potatoes
3 medium sized tomatoes

45 ml ghee
1 tsp mustard seeds
1 tsp cumin seeds
1 tsp asafetida
4 curry leaves
2 chopped green chillies
2 tbs grated ginger
1 tsp turmeric
1 ½ tsp salt
⅓ tsp garam masala
sprinkle lemon juice
fresh coriander leaves

Preparation Method

Choose karelas (6), wash cut into thin rings and collect in a large colander and set aside.

Wash and peel medium sized potatoes (2-3), cut into cubes and set aside in another colander.

Next take tomatoes (3) wash and cut into cubes. Leave to stand on the chopping board.

Fill a karhai / wok or deep-frying pan three quarters with ghee and heat over a medium heat.

Line a colander with kitchen roll to remove excess ghee.

Add the karela rings in small handfuls at a time to prevent ghee from over flowing. Deep-fry on a medium flame until the karelas are crispy looking.

Transfer the fried karela to the lined colander.

On a slightly lower flame deep-fry the potatoes. Remove the fried potatoes with slotted spoon drain off the excess ghee transfer them to a different colander which is also lined with kitchen roll to soak up excess ghee. Move on to making the masala.

Add ghee (1 ladle 45 ml), to a large saucepan over a medium flame. Toss in mustard seeds (1 tsp) and allow them pop.

Next add cumin seeds (1 tsp), asafetida (1 tsp), dry curry leaves (4), chopped chillies (2), grated ginger (2 tbs) and the cubed tomatoes (3).

Cook for 1-2 minutes now introduce the fried potatoes and ring shape crispy karela from the colanders.

Add turmeric (1 tsp), salt (1 ½ tsp) and garam masala (⅓ tsp). Mix once or twice with a stainless steel spoon, sprinkle with lemon juice and garnish with washed, finely chopped coriander leaves and serve.

Preparation time: 15 min   Frying time: 20 min

Ingredients

12 small sized karelas
10 cm in length
¾ tsp salt
1 ½ cups chickpea flour
4 ½ tbs dhana jeera
2 ½ tsp salt
1 ½ tsp turmeric
3 tbs sugar
1 ½ tsp lemon juice
3 tbs oil
100 ml water approx

65 ml ghee
1 ½ tsp mustard seeds
1 tbs grated ginger
1-2 chopped green chillies
1 ½ tsp asfetida
½ tsp turmeric

Preparation Method

Choose smaller sized karelas (12) not more than 10 cm in length.

Remove the bitterness of karela by gently scraping the outside with a potato peeler.

Next cut the karelas into 3 cm rings and place in a medium sized pot filled with water and salt (¾ tsp). Bring to the boil over a medium flame for 10-15 minutes until the karelas are half cooked.

Stuffing

Next in a small saucepan dry roast chickpea flour (1 ½ cups) over a medium flame for 5 minutes.

Take the pot off the heat and transfer the roasted chickpea flour to a small mixing bowl.

Add dhana jeera (4 ½ tbs), salt (2 ½ tsp), turmeric (1 ½ tsp), sugar (3 tbs), lemon juice (1 ½ tsp), oil (3 tbs) and water (100 ml) which will help to bind all the ingredients.

Return to the boiling karela, turn off the flame and carefully drain the water through a colander.

Allow the karela pieces to cool down. When cool enough to handle, remove the centre of each ring shaped karela with a knife or spoon and fill with the seasoned chickpea flour. Place all the stuffed karelas on a chopping board.

In a medium sized non-stick wok add ghee (1 medium sized ladle 65 ml) and mustard seeds (1 ½ tsp). Allow the seeds to pop next add asafetida (1 ½ tsp), grated ginger (1 tbs), chopped green chillies (1-2), turmeric (½ tsp) and mix.

Next add the stuffed ring karelas carefully so as not to disturb the stuffing. Cover and cook over a medium flame for a further 5 minutes without stirring and serve.

Preparation time: 10 min   Boiling and cooking time: 20 min   Stuffing time: 15 min

4.7 PUMPKIN AND PANEER

Ingredients

1.2 kg pumpkin
2.2 litres full fat milk
180 ml bottled lemon juice

45 ml ghee
2 dry red chillies
2 tsp cumin seeds
2 bay leaves
½ tsp asafetida
½ tsp turmeric
1 ½ tsp salt
fresh coriander leaves

Preparation Method

First make the cubed paneer as described in recipe 3.2 from full fat milk (2.2 litres) and bottled lemon juice (180 ml).

Take one pumpkin (1.2 kg) cut in half remove the seeds and discard.

After peeling cut the pumpkin halves into medium sized cubes. Set aside in a colander.

Add ghee (1 ladle 45 ml) to a large saucepan over a medium flame. Next add dry red chillies (2) and cumin seeds (2 tsp), allow cumin seeds to sizzle now add bay leaves (2), followed by asafetida (½ tsp), then turmeric (½ tsp) and salt (1 ½ tsp).

Introduce the cubed pumpkin to the mixture of spices and mix. Cook for 15 minutes.

There is no need to add any extra water as the pumpkin releases water.

At the end of this cooking period add the cubed paneer (not fried).

Stir for 5 minutes with a stainless steel spoon. Garnish with washed and freshly cut coriander leaves and serve.

Preparation time: 20 min   Cooking time: 20 min

N.B. Pumpkin can be with replaced with butternut squash (1.2 kg).

4.8 OKRA / BHINDI (LADY FINGERS) WITH POTATOES

Ingredients

1 kg okra approximately
4 medium sized potatoes

45 ml ghee
1 tsp mustard seeds
1 tsp cumin seeds
2 tbs grated ginger
2 chopped green chillies
1 tsp asafetida
1 tsp turmeric
1- 1 ½ tsp garam masala
1 ½ tsp salt

Preparation Method

Weigh out approximately 1 kg of okra and add to a colander.

Wash, top and tail and pat dry the okra using a tea towel to remove water which causes stickiness during cooking.

After drying slice the okra into 1-1 ½ cm rings. Discard any pieces which might have food spoilage present.

Wash and peel potatoes (4) and cut into small cubes similar in size to the okra slices.

Add ghee (1 ladle 45 ml) to a large non-stick saucepan and heat over a medium flame.

Toss in mustard seeds (1 tsp) and wait for them to pop.

Next add cumin seeds (1 tsp) allow to sizzle then add grated ginger (2 tbs), chopped green chillies (2), asafetida (1 tsp) and mix. Next add the cubed potatoes, followed by turmeric (1 tsp), garam masala (1-1 ½ tsp) and finally salt (1 ½ tsp). Cook for 5 minutes. Now add the sliced okra and mix with a wooden spoon. **Do not add extra water,** okra must be cooked dry any addition of water will make them sticky.

Place a lid upside down over the open saucepan and add water (½ cup) to the lid. This helps with the cooking process and prevents burning. Cook slowly for 20 minutes and serve.

Preparation time: 20 min   Cooking time: 25 min

4.9 Deep-Fried Chip Shaped Potatoes and Chip Shaped Okra

Ingredients

1 kg okra
4 potatoes
1 tomato

45 ml ghee
3 tbs punch pooran
½ tsp asafetida
2 tbs grated ginger
2 chopped green chillies
1 tsp turmeric
1 ½ tsp salt

Preparation Method

Weigh out okra (1 kg) or fill a large flat topped colander.

Wash the okra and pat dry with a tea towel.

Top and tail the dried okra and cut into chip like shapes. Discard any pieces which might have food spoilage present.

Choose potatoes (4 large) wash, peel and cut into chips.

Line two flat topped colanders with kitchen roll to absorb excess ghee after frying.

Fill a karhai / wok or deep-frying pan three quarters with ghee and deep-fry the chips first over a medium flame. Remove the fried chips with a slotted spoon and put them into the lined colander and set aside.

Next deep-fry the chipped shaped okra pieces and after frying remove the fried okra with a slotted spoon and place them into the other lined colander.

Move on to making the masala. Add ghee (45 ml) to a non-stick wok and heat over a medium flame.

Toss in punch pooran (3 tbs), asafetida (½ tsp), grated ginger (2 tbs), chopped green chillies (2), followed by the fried okra and potatoes. Add turmeric (1 tsp) and salt (1 ½ tsp). To finish off add one chopped tomato mix with a stainless steel spoon and serve.

Preparation time: 20 min   Frying time: 20 min

4.10 Stuffed baby aubergines

Ingredients

12-18 baby aubergines
3-4 cubed tomatoes
1.7 litres milk
140 ml bottled lemon juice

45 ml ghee
1 tsp mustard seeds
1 tsp cumin seeds
2 tbs grated ginger
2 green chillies
½ tsp asafetida
½ tsp turmeric
1 tsp paprika powder
¾ tsp salt

Spices for filling
30 ml ghee
1 tsp mustard seeds
1 tsp cumin seeds
½ tsp dhana jeera
½ tsp paprika powder
½ tsp garam masala
¾ tsp salt

Preparation Method

Pick out baby aubergines (12-16) which should be no longer than 10 cm.

Wash and remove the stems.

Score the base of the baby aubergine in a crisscross pattern and then cut the aubergine into four quarters, up to three quarters the length of the baby aubergines taking care not to cut right through the top.

This allows the split aubergines to open like a flower in preparation ready for filling.

Filling preparation

Prepare paneer as described in section 3.2 using full fat milk (1.7 litres) and bottled lemon juice (140 ml). Press under a heavy weight for five minutes. Here loose paneer is preferred for the filling.

Remove the paneer from the cheese cloth and transfer to a medium sized mixing bowl for spicing.

Make the chaunce (spice mixture) in a small pot over a medium flame.

Spoon in ghee (30 ml), add mustard seeds (1 tsp) and allow the seeds to pop.

Next add cumin seeds (1 tsp), dhana jeera (½ tsp), paprika powder (½ tsp) and garam masala (½ tsp). Cook for 1-2 minutes then pour the mixture on top of the paneer and add salt (¾ tsp).

Mix the chaunce and the paneer by hand thoroughly. Be careful as the chaunce will be hot.

If the texture is dry add blended tomato (1) or if the paneer is too wet add milk powder (1 tbs) to adjust the texture.

Add the filling to the split aubergines removing excess filling around the top and sides. The filled aubergines are placed on a stainless steel tray.

Next add ghee (1 ladle 45 ml) to a large non-stick wok and heat over a medium flame. Toss in mustard seeds (1 tsp) and let the seeds pop now add cumin seeds (1 tsp), grated ginger (2 tbs), chopped green chillies (2), asafetida (½ tsp), turmeric (1 tsp), paprika powder (1 tsp), followed by washed and cubed tomatoes (3-4). Mix and cook for 1-2 minutes.

Place the stuffed baby aubergines into the wok, sprinkle with salt (¾ tsp) cover with a lid and cook for 20 minutes in their juices.

Do not mix, only shake the wok. If you really need to turn the stuffed aubergines then do so only with chapati tongs, otherwise do not disturb the cooking procees. Stuffed baby aubergines can easily disintegrate.

Once cooked remove carefully and serve.

Preparation time: 25 min   Cooking time: 20 min

Ingredients

3 karelas
½ butternut squash
2 medium sized potatoes
1 aubergine
3-4 cooking bananas (matoki)
1 drumstick (optional)

45 ml ghee
2 tbs punch pooran
1 chopped green chilli
2 tbs grated ginger
¾ tsp asafetida
½ tsp turmeric
1 ½ tsp salt
2 tsp mustard seeds roasted then ground

Preparation Method

Take karelas (3), wash and cut into cubes. Next choose one aubergine, remove the stems wash and cut into cubes. Combine both the cubed karela and aubergine in one large sized colander.

Next wash peel and cut into cubes butternut squash (½), cooking bananas / matoki (3-4) and potatoes (2 medium sized).

Keep the potato cubes in a separate colander. Combine all the other cut vegetables in either 1-2 colanders.

As an optional extra, use one drumstick which has been washed and scraped gently with a potato peeler. Cut the drumstick into 3 cm pieces and set aside.

Add ghee (1 ladle 45 ml) to a non-stick wok and stand over a medium flame.

Add punch pooran (2 tbs) which is a blend of 5 spices (cumin, fenugreek, fennel, kalonji and mustard seeds) to the ghee followed by chopped chillies (1), grated ginger (2 tbs) and asafetida (¾ tsp).

To the mixture of spices add the cubed potatoes first and cook for 5 minutes on their own. Next add all the remaining vegetables followed by turmeric (½ tsp) and salt (1 ½ tsp).

Mix with a wooden spoon, cover with a lid and cook for 15 minutes.

During the cooking period take mustard seeds (2 tsp) and dry roast them on a hot tava or a small pot until they begin to pop. At this point transfer them to a coffee grinder and grind to a fine powder. If a coffee grinder is not available crush on the kitchen work-top with a rolling pin. At the end of the cooking period add the crushed mustard seeds and mix.

Potatoes take longer to cook. To check if they are cooked, cut a potato into 2 pieces with a knife if this occurs easily the dry sukta is ready to be served.

Preparation time: 15 min   Cooking time: 20 min

4.12 PARWAR (POTOLS) AND POTATOES

Ingredients

800 g parwar (potols)
2-3 medium sized potatoes
1 large tomato

45 ml ghee
2 tbs punch pooran
¾ tsp asafetida
2 chopped green chillies
2 tbs grated ginger
1 ½ tsp salt
1 tsp turmeric
2 tsp mustard powder

Preparation Method

Wash, top and tail parwar / potols (800 g).

Cut each parwar lengthwise to give two equal halves add to a large colander and set aside.

Next take potatoes (2), wash, peel, cut into cubes and set aside.

To a large wok over a medium flame add ghee (1 ladle 45 ml).

Next add to the warming ghee punch pooran (2 tbs), asafetida (¾ tsp), chopped green chillies (2) and grated ginger (2 tbs).

Mix with a wooden spoon, now add the cubed potatoes (2-3) and parwar halves.

Continue flavouring with salt (1 ½ tsp) and turmeric (1 tsp).

Stir, cover with a lid and cook for 15 minutes. At the end of the cooking add ground mustard powder (2 tsp).

The sabji is cooked when the potatoes are cooked. Cut one potato in half with a knife, if is easily cut the sabji is ready.

Before serving add one large washed cubed tomato to the cooked vegetables. Mix once and serve.

Preparation time: 15 min   Cooking time: 15 min

N.B. A second way of cooking this parwar and potatoes sabji is to deep-fry them separately in a kharai / wok or deep-frying pan filled three quarters with ghee over a medium flame.

First deep-fry the cubed potatoes remove with a slotted spoon and set aside in a colander lined with kitchen roll to absorb excess ghee.

Cut each parwar into 1 cm rings approximately 3 segments per parwar deep-fry remove from the ghee with a slotted spoon shake off as much ghee as possible then add to the fried potatoes in the mentioned colander.

In a medium sized pot over a medium flame add ghee (1 ladle 45 ml), punch pooran (2 tbs), asafetida (¾ tsp), chopped green chillies (2) and grated ginger. Stir and now add the fried vegetables followed by salt (1 ½ tsp), turmeric (1 tsp) and finally mustard powder (2 tsp). Mix and serve.

Preparation time: 15 min   Frying time: 15 min

Ingredients

2 kg potatoes
1 bunch fresh methi

45 ml ghee
1 tbs mustard seeds
2 green chillies
1 tbs grated fresh ginger
½ tsp asafetida
1 ½ tsp turmeric
1 tsp garam masala
1 ½ tsp salt
2 tbs lemon juice

Preparation Method

Wash, peel and cut into wedges potatoes (2 kg).

Place the wedges in a large mixing bowl and marinate in turmeric (1 ½ tsp) and set aside for 5 minutes.

Take a fresh bunch of methi, either remove all the leaves discarding the stems and set aside or finely chop the entire bunch discarding the bottom ends.

To a non-stick saucepan over a medium flame add ghee (1 ladle 45 ml) and mustard seeds (1 tbs).

Allow the mustard seeds to pop. Next add finely chopped green chillies (2), grated fresh ginger (1 tbs), followed by asafetida (½ tsp).

Next add all the marinated potatoes followed by the garam masala (½ tsp) and salt (1 ½ tsp).

Cook for 15 minutes on a low flame without any addition of water.

When the potatoes are almost cooked add either fresh methi leaves or finely chopped bunch of methi. Mix cook for a further 5 minutes and at the end sprinkle with lemon juice and serve.

Preparation time: 10 min   Cooking time: 20 min

4.14 Tindora

Ingredients

800 g-1 kg tindora
2 medium sized potatoes
2 tomatoes

65 ml ghee
1 tsp mustard seeds
1 tsp asafetida
2 green chillies
1 tbs grated ginger
1 tbs dhana jeera
1 tsp turmeric
1 ½ tsp salt
½ bunch fresh coriander leaves

Preparation Method

Wash, top and tail tindora (800 g-1 kg) and cut into long strips.

Next wash and peel medium sized potatoes (2), cut in small cubes. Slice tomatoes (2) into wedges and set aside.

To a medium sized wok add ghee (1 medium ladle 65 ml), mustard seeds (1 tsp) and allow them to pop. Next add asafetida (1 tsp), finely chopped green chillies (2) and grated fresh ginger (1 tbs).

Now add the prepared tindora and the cubed potatoes, followed by dhana jeera (1 tbs), turmeric (1 tsp) and salt (1 ½ tsp). Add water (⅓ cup) if needed to prevent burning. Cover with a lid and cook over a medium flame for 15-20 minutes.

Add the sliced tomatoes (2), mix with a stainless steel spoon, garnish with washed, finely chopped coriander leaves and serve.

Preparation time: 25 min   Cooking time: 20 min

4.15 GREEN FRENCH BEANS WITH EITHER POTATOES OR PANEER

Ingredients

600 g French beans
2-3 medium potatoes
2 litres full fat milk
160 ml bottled lemon juice

45 ml ghee
1 tsp mustard seeds
1 tsp cumin seeds
1 tsp asafetida
2 green chillies
1 tbs grated fresh ginger
1 ½ tsp salt
1 tsp turmeric

Preparation Method

French beans (600 g) are washed, top and tailed, cut into two equal pieces and set aside in a flat topped colander. Medium sized potatoes (2-3) are washed, peeled, cut into small cubes and added to the French beans.

To a medium sized saucepan, over a medium flame add ghee (1 ladle 45 ml) and mustard seeds. Allow the seeds to pop, next add add cumin seeds (1 tsp), asafetida (1 tsp), finely chopped green chillies (2) and grated fresh ginger (1 tbs).

Next add the prepared vegetables followed by salt (1 ½ tsp) and turmeric (1 tsp). Cover with a lid and allow to cook for 15-20 minutes and serve.

Instead of potatoes add plain paneer at the end of the 20 minutes cooking time stir and serve.

Make the cubed paneeer from full fat milk (2 litres) and bottled lemon juice (160 ml), see recipe 3.2.

Preparation time: 10 min   Cooking time: 20 min

Ingredients

800 g-1 kg valor
1 large aubergine
½-1 cup frozen peas
2-3 blended tomatoes

65 ml ghee
1 tsp mustard seeds
1 tsp ajwain seeds
1 tsp asafetida
1 tsp turmeric
1 tsp chilli powder
2 tbs dhana jeera
1 ½ tsp salt
1-2 tsp sugar

Preparation Method

Valor (800 g-1 kg) are washed then top and tailed. Remove the stringy outer edge and discard. Open the valor to give two halves. Cut each half diagonally into 2-3 pieces.

A large aubergine is washed, cut into medium sized cubes and set aside.

Measure out frozen peas (¾ cup) into a sieve wash with hot water and set aside.

To a large pot over a medium flame add ghee (1 medium ladle 65 ml), toss in mustard seeds (1 tsp) and allow them to pop, then add ajwain seeds (1 tsp), asafetida (1 tsp), followed by the above mentioned vegetables. Rapidly add turmeric (1 tsp), chilli powder (1 tsp), dhana jeera (2 tbs), salt (1 ½ tsp) and sugar (1-2 tsp).

Mix and cover with a lid. Cook over a medium flame for 15 minutes. When cooked add blended tomatoes (2-3). Cook for a further 5 minutes and serve or garnish with washed, finely chopped coriander leaves and serve.

Preparation time: 20 min   Cooking time: 20 min

4.17 GUVAR AND MUTHIA

Ingredients

800 g guvar
½ bunch fresh coriander
2 tbs lemon juice

65 ml ghee
1 tsp mustard seeds
1 tsp ajwain seeds
1 tsp asafetida
½ tsp turmeric
1 tsp chilli powder
1 tbs dhana jeera
2 tsp salt
¼ tsp bicarbonate soda
2 cups water
1 tbs jaggery

Mixture for muthia
1 ½ cups chickpea flour
1 tsp salt
2 tsp sugar
1 tbs oil
¼ tsp bicarbonate soda
1 tbs lemon juice
½ bunch methi
¼ cup water approx

Preparation Method

Guvar (800 g) is washed, top and tailed cut in half and set aside in a large flat topped colander. The **first part** of this recipe is cooking guvar **without the muthia.**

To a large pot, over a medium flame, add ghee (1 medium ladle 65 ml) toss in mustard seeds (1 tsp) and allow them to pop. Next add ajwain seeds (1 tsp), asafetida (1 tsp) and the prepared guvar.

Continue spicing with, turmeric (½ tsp), chilli powder (1 tsp), dhana jeera (1 tbs), salt (2 tsp), bicarbonate soda (¼ tsp) and water (2 cups). Cover with a lid and cook over a medium flame for 15 minutes then add blended tomatoes (3) mix, add jaggery (1 tbs) garnish with chopped coriander leaves and serve. To make guvar **with muthias** follow above but do not add blended tomatoes.

Preparation of muthia also known as chickpea flour dumplings mixed with fresh methi leaves.

While the guvar is cooking make muthias / dumplings, which are small balls (2 cm) in diameter.

To a mixing bowl add chickpea flour (1 ½ cup), salt (1 tsp), sugar (2 tsp), oil (1 tbs), bicarbonate soda (¼ tsp), lemon juice (1 tbs), half a bunch of washed and finely chopped methi plus water (¼ cup approximately).

Mix by hand and make as many dumplings as possible by rolling the chickpea flour mixture between the palms of your hands. Collect on a stainless steel tray and set aside.

Line a colander with a kitchen towel to soak up excess ghee.

Fry the balls in a karhai / wok or deep-frying pan three quarters filled with ghee over a medium flame until golden. Remove the balls with a slotted spoon and place into the lined colander. After draining add the fried balls directly into the guvar sabji and continue to cook for a further 5 minutes and mix.
Garnish with washed, finely chopped coriander leaves, sprinkle with lemon juice (2 tbs) and serve.

Preparation time: 20 min   Cooking time: 20 min   Frying time: 10 min

Ingredients

5 courgettes
5 litres full fat milk
425 ml bottled lemon juice
5 medium sized tomatoes
½ bunch fresh coriander

45 ml ghee
½ tsp mustard seeds
½ tsp asafetida
2 green chillies
2 tbs grated fresh ginger
2 tsp dhana jeera
½ tsp turmeric
1 ½ tsp salt
1 ½ tsp garam masala

Preparation Method

Cubed paneer is prepared as described in recipe 3.2 using full fat milk (5 litres) and bottled lemon juice (425 ml).

Wash and cut the courgettes (5) into cubes and set aside.

To a large saucepan over a medium flame add ghee (1 ½ ladle 45 ml). Toss in mustard seeds (½ tsp) and allow them to pop.

Next add asafetida (½ tsp) finely chopped green chillies (2), freshly grated ginger (2 tbs) and mix. Introduce the cubed courgettes and cook for 10 minutes until the courgettes soften.

Meanwhile in a karhai / wok or deep-frying pan, over a medium flame, fill three quarters with ghee and deep-fry the cubed paneer to golden brown.

Remove the fried paneer cubes with a slotted spoon and immerse in a bowl of hot water with salt (½ tsp) and turmeric (½ tsp) or immerse the fried paneer cubes in a bowl of whey for 5-10 minutes.

The fried paneer is removed from the water with a slotted spoon drained and added to the cooking courgettes. Add dhana jeera (2 tsp), turmeric (½ tsp) and salt (1 ½ tsp).

Cook in its juices for a further 5 minutes with chopped tomatoes (5), add garam masala (1 ½ tsp), mix and serve with or without washed freshly chopped coriander leaves as a garnish.

Preparation time: 20 min   Frying time: 5 min   Cooking time: 15 min

Ingredients

1 kg Brussels sprouts
2 large potatoes
1 red pepper

45 ml ghee
1 tsp mustard seeds
1 tsp fenugreek
1 tsp cumin seeds
1 tbs grated ginger
1 tsp asafetida
1 ½ tsp salt
1 tsp turmeric
½ tsp black pepper

Preparation Method

Wash and prepare Brussels sprouts (1 kg) by removing old and damaged leaves.

Score the bottom of the Brussels sprouts in a crisscross pattern and set aside in a colander.

Wash and peel large potatoes (2) cut into cubes and set aside.

Wash cut into half, red pepper (1) remove the seeds and cut into cubes.

Line the colander with kitchen roll to absorb excess ghee.

Set up a karhai / wok or a deep-frying pan, fill three quarters with ghee and heat over a medium flame.

First deep-fry the Brussels sprouts until golden brown. Remove with a slotted spoon and set aside in the lined colander. Next deep-fry the potatoes. Remove with a slotted spoon. Tap the slotted spoon on the side of the karhai to remove excess ghee and combine with the Brussels sprouts.

Move on to make the masala.

To a saucepan over a medium flame add ghee (1 small ladle 45 ml).

Toss in mustard seeds (1 tsp), allow them to pop then add fenugreek seeds (1 tsp), cumin seeds (1 tsp), grated ginger (1 tbs) and asafetida (1 tsp) followed by cubed red pepper and cook for 2-3 minutes.

Add the fried Brussels sprouts and potatoes to the masala followed by salt (1 ½ tsp), turmeric (1 tsp) and black pepper (½ tsp).

Mix well with a stainless steel spoon and serve.

Preparation time: 20 min   Frying time: 20 min

Ingredients

2 large aubergines
3-4 medium sized courgettes
1 yellow pepper
1 red pepper
4 medium sized tomatoes
1 small packet basil or
1 tbs mixed herbs

60 ml olive oil
1 tsp asafetida
½ tsp black pepper
1 ½ tsp salt

Preparation Method

Wash aubergines (2) and cut into 2 cm cubes and set aside in a colander. Sprinkle with salt and marinate for 10-20 minutes.

Wash and cut into cubes courgettes (4), yellow and red pepper (1 of each). Set aside in another colander.

Return to the aubergines wash away the salt and dry the cubed aubergines in a tea towel.

In a large saucepan or wok heat olive oil (60 ml) over a medium flame.

Add asafetida (1 tsp) and introduce the cubed aubergines. Cook for 3-5 minutes.

Next add the cubed courgettes and peppers followed by salt (1 ½ tsp), black pepper (½ tsp).

Mix with a wooden spoon, cover and cook for 15 minutes without water.

Take medium sized tomatoes (3-4) cut into cubes and add to the cooked mixture of vegetables.

Mix and continue cooking for 5 more minutes.

Garnish with washed and chopped basil (1 packet) or sprinkle with mixed herbs (1 tbs) and serve.

Preparation time: 10 min   Cooking time: 15 min

BREADS

Ingredients

4 cups medium chapati flour
2 tbs oil
1 tsp salt
1 ⅓ cups hot water (approx)

Preparation Method

To a large mixing bowl add chapati flour (4 cups).

If chapati flour is not available a mixture of brown flour (3 cups) and white flour
(1 cup) can be used.

Make a small well in the mound of flour and fill with oil (2 tbs), followed by salt (1 tsp).

Add hot water (1 ⅓ cups) and begin to mix with your hands. If more water is needed only add small amounts to help with the kneading.

Try to gather all the flour around the edges of the bowl. Turn the dough out onto the work surface and continue kneading for 5 minutes until the dough is smooth and firm.

Shape the dough to look like a French roll (30-35 cm long). Divide the length first into half then quarters and then each quarter into four equal sized portions to give a total of 16 pieces.

Cover the 16 pieces with a tea-towel to keep moist.

Sprinkle the working surface with chapati flour and from the 16 pieces make perfectly rounded mini balls between the palms of your hands and flatten.

Dip them into a heap of flour and roll each one using either a standard wooden or a chapati rolling pin. Make them as round as possible (approximately 20 cm) across. As you roll, pick the chapati up and turn clockwise to shape them into perfectly rounded chapatis. Keep dusting with flour to prevent sticking to the surface.

Place two tavas or heavy cast-iron griddle over a medium flame in preparation for cooking the rolled out chapatis.

Remove excess flour from the rolled chapati and place first on the preheated tavas.

When small white blisters appear on the surface of the chapati and the edges begin to curl up turn the chapati over with a pair of flat tongs and cook the other side until the surface bulges with small air pockets.

Lift the chapati with metal tongs and then place directly over a flame for few seconds, then turn the chapati over until it inflates like a balloon.

A finished chapati should be cooked completely and should be freckled with brown spots on either sides. Press the air out while covering the surface with butter.

Fold each cooked chapati into a triangular shape and serve with sabjis. Chapatis can also be cooked on an electric cooker. Place the rolled out chapati on a hot tava or frying pan placed on top of the hot plate. Turn the cooking chapati over several times, press gently with a soft cloth until it inflates. Remove, cover with butter and serve.

Preparation and rolling time: 15 min   Cooking time: 15 min

Ingredients

2 cups self raising flour
1 cup medium chapati flour
80 ml yogurt
1 cup hot water (approximately)

1 tsp kalonji seeds (optional)
1 tsp salt
½ tsp turmeric
1 tbs oil

Preparation Method

To a mixing bowl add self raising flour (2 cups) and chapati flour (1 cup).

Next add oil (1 tbs), salt (1 tsp), turmeric (½ tsp), kalonji seeds, optional (1 tsp), plain yogurt (80 ml) and hot water approximately (1 cup).

Mix well by hand to give a yellow coloured dough. Continue the kneading process on the work surface and shape into a French roll (30-35 cm) long.

Divide into 16 smaller pieces see chapati recipe 5.1. Cover the small balls with a tea towel.

To prevent sticking when rolling spread a little oil on the table.

Each ball is rounded in between the palms of your hands and then flatten.

Using either a small wooden rolling pin or a chapati rolling pin, roll the flattened balls into 10 cm circles.

Line a colander with kitchen roll to absorb excess ghee.

Fill a karhai / wok or deep-frying pan three quarters with ghee and heat over a high flame.

When the ghee begins to almost smoke lower to a medium flame.

Place a puri on the surface of the ghee being careful not to burn your fingers.

The puri will sink to the bottom of the ghee and then rise to the surface.

Immediately submerge the puri gently below the surface of the ghee until it begins to inflate like a balloon. Use a slotted spoon to press it down. Gradually allow the puri to rise to the surface of the hot ghee.

Fry the other side for a few seconds, remove with a slotted spoon, drain the ghee by tapping on the top of the deep-frying pan to remove excess ghee, and place the fried puri on its edge in the colander lined with kitchen towel.

Repeat this procedure with the remainder of puris.

Transfer the puris to plates and serve.

Preparation and rolling time: 15 min   Frying time: 15 min

5.3 PARATHA

Ingredients

4 ½ cups medium chapati flour
1 ⅓ cups hot water

2 tbs melted ghee
1 ½ tsp salt

Preparation Method

To a large mixing bowl add medium chapati flour (4 ½ cups).

If chapati flour is not available use a mixture of brown flour (3 ¼ cups) and white flour (1 ¼ cup).

Make a small well in the mound of flour. Pour melted ghee (2 tbs) into the middle followed by the addition of salt (1 ½ tsp) and then hot water (1 ⅓ cups).

Mix with your hands and prepare the dough to a medium stiff texture.

Continue the kneading process on the work surface and shape into a French roll (30-35 cm).

Divide the dough into half then into four quarters and each quarter is divided into four to give total of 16 equal sized pieces which are shaped into rounded balls in between the palms of your hands and flattened. Cover with a tea towel to keep moist.

Place two tavas or heavy cast iron griddle over a medium flame ready for cooking.

Dust the work surface with flour to prevent sticking to the kitchen work surface. Roll the flattened balls into circles (10 cm diameter).

Brush the surface of each disc with melted ghee and fold it in half. Butter the surface again and fold each paratha in half a second time making triangles. Roll the parathas thinly into large triangles.

Place a paratha on the preheated tava or griddle and cook evenly over a medium flame which do take longer to cook than chapatis.

When both sides are golden brown rub ghee (½ tsp) on the surface and spread the ghee evenly using the back of the spoon. Press down hard with the spoon and then turn the paratha over add more ghee and spread evenly and at the same time pressing down hard on the surface.

The parathas should puff up on pressing down on its surface and is complete when both sides are golden brown and flecked with dark spots.

When all the parathas are cooked serve with a sabji.

Preparation time: 15 min   Rolling and cooking time: 25 min

SAVOURIES

6.1 Pakora (vegetable fritters)

Ingredients

1 large cauliflower (1 kg)

1 ½ cup chickpea flour
1 tsp salt
1 tsp kalonji seeds
1 ½ tsp dhana jeera powder
½ tsp asafetida
½ tsp chilli powder
1 tsp turmeric
approx 1 cup water

Preparation Method

Wash and trim one large cauliflower and cut into 20 equal sized medium florets. Collect all the cut pieces in a flat surfaced colander and set aside.

Mix chickpea flour (1 ½ cups) with salt (1 tsp), kalonji seeds (1 tsp), dhana jeera powder (1 ½ tsp), asafetida (½ tsp), chilli powder (½ tsp) and turmeric (1 tsp) in a bowl.

Next add warm water approximately (1 cup) and whisk until you get a smooth batter, free of lumps and thick enough to coat the vegetables. Take care not to make the batter too runny or thick. Add either water or more chickpea flour to adjust the texture. A perfect texture is similar to "wall paper glue".

Line a colander with kitchen roll to absorb excess ghee.

Fill a karhai / wok, or a deep-frying pan three quarters full with ghee and heat over a medium flame.

The ghee is hot enough when a drop of batter added rises immediately to the surface and sizzles.

It is important not to have the ghee very hot which would rapidly cook the surrounding batter leaving the cauliflower raw.

Soak the florets of cauliflower (20) either all or individually in the batter.

Take the coated cauliflower pieces out of the batter one by one and place them quickly into the hot ghee until the surface of the ghee is covered.

Deep-fry for several minutes until the batter turns golden brown. Use a slotted spoon to turn the pakoras over during frying.

Pierce the pakora with a small sharp knife to see if the cauliflower is cooked. If the cauliflower is easily pierced remove the pakoras from the ghee, drain and transfer to the lined colander.

Transfer the pakoras to plates and serve with one of the following chutneys: cooked or fresh tomato chutney, fruit, tamarind or avocado chutney.

Instead of cauliflower sliced aubergines, potatoes, coloured peppers and courgette rings can be used.

Paneer prepared as described in 3.2 can be cut into approximately 4 cm x 4 cm squares, dip into the batter and fry to make paneer pakoras.

Preparation time: 10 min   Frying time: 15 min

6.2 MASHED POTATO PAKORAS

Ingredients

0.8 kg red potatoes

1 ½ cup chickpea flour
1 ½ tsp salt
2 chopped green chillies
2 tbs grated ginger
2 tbs lemon juice
½ bunch fresh chopped
coriander leaves
⅓ tsp cinnamon powder
1 tsp turmeric
1 tbs ghee
1 tsp mustard seeds
¾ tsp asafetida

Preparation Method

First wash red potatoes (0.8 kg) and boil them in a large pot of water over a medium flame for (approximately 30-45 minutes).

Remove the pot from the heat and carefully drain. Allow the potatoes to cool to room temperature and then remove the skin.

Place the peeled potatoes in a large mixing bowl and mash. Add salt (1 ½ tsp), chopped green chillies (2), grated ginger (2 tbs), lemon juice (2 tbs) and freshly cut and washed coriander leaves (½ a bunch), cinnamon powder (⅓ tsp) and turmeric (1 tsp) to the mashed potatoes.

In a small ladle or small pot over a high flame make the chaunce (mixture of spices) with ghee (1 tbs) mustard seeds (1 tsp) and asafetida (¾ tsp).

Immediately after sizzling, pour the chaunce on top of the spiced mountain of mashed potatoes.

Mix by hand. Take care with the hot chaunce. After mixing make 16 equal sized balls and place on a tray.

Prepare chickpea flour batter as described in making cauliflower pakora 6.1.

Line the base of a colander with kitchen roll to absorb excess ghee.

Coat each spiced potato ball with batter and deep-fry in the same manner as described in 6.1.

When all 16 balls have been fried remove the balls with slotted spoon drain excess ghee and transfer to the lined colander.

Place the mashed potatoes pakoras carefully on plates and serve with cooked or fresh tomato chutney, coriander, tamarind or avocado chutney.

Preparation time: 10-15 min   Boiling time: 30 min   Frying time: 15 min

Ingredients

1 cauliflower (600-800 g)
2 cups frozen peas
1 red pepper
2 potatoes (200 g)

45 ml ghee
2 tbs cumin seeds
2 ½ tbs grated ginger
2 green chillies
1 ½ tsp asafetida
1 tsp turmeric
½ tsp cinnamon powder
1 ½ tsp salt
1 tsp lemon juice
¼ bunch chopped
coriander leaves

Pastry for 16 samosas
3 cups plain flour
½ cup chapati flour
1 ½ tsp salt
8 tbs or ½ cup melted ghee
1 cup hot water

Preparation Method

Wash and cut a cauliflower (approximately 600-800 g) into small florets (1 ½ cm) and set aside in a flat topped colander.

Wash and cut a red pepper into half, remove the seeds and continue cutting the red pepper into small pieces keeping them similar in size to the cauliflower pieces.

Wash, peel and dice one large or two medium sized potatoes (200 g) into small cubes the same size as the cauliflower and the red pepper.

Measure out frozen peas (2 cups) into a sieve, wash with hot water and add to the diced red pepper, potatoes and cauliflower.

To a large non-stick wok over a medium heat add ghee (1 small ladle 45 ml) followed by cumin seeds (2 tbs), grated ginger (2 ½ tbs), finely chopped green chillies (2) and asafetida (1 ½ tsp).

Stir this mixture of spices and cook for about 1 minute.

Add the vegetables to the spice mixture followed by a second set of spices turmeric (1 tsp), ground cinnamon powder (½ tsp) and salt (1 ½ tsp).

Mix and cook for 15 minutes.

At the end of the cooking sprinkle lemon juice and finely chopped washed coriander leaves (¼ bunch).

Transfer the filling from the wok into a (20 cm x 30 cm) oblong cake pan and spread evenly or leave the filling in the wok and allow to cool.

While the filling is cooling prepare the pastry in a mixing bowl with plain flour (3 cups) chapati flour (½ cup), salt (1 ½ tsp), melted ghee (8 tbs or ½ cup) and hot water (1 cup).

Mix by hand for 5 minutes until the dough is soft and smooth. Empty the dough onto the work top. Continue kneading by pushing back and forth with both hands and then shape the dough into a French loaf (30-35 cm) long.

Cut the dough into eight equal portions and make balls. Cover with a damp cloth and set aside. Return to the cold filling and divide it into 16 equal portions. With a plastic spatula first make a cross in the filling to give 4 equal quarters. Next cut two lines an either side of the centre vertical line followed by two lines on either side of the horizontal middle line. This will give 16 equal portions.

Next roll each rounded dough piece into a circle (15-20 cm) in diameter and cut each circle into half.

Take each half-circle and moisten the edge of the straight side with a little water using your finger. Bring the two ends of the straight side together and overlap them by ½ cm to make a cone.

Firmly press the dry side over the wet side to seal the cone tight or without using water overlap the two ends and press them firmly so that they do not open up when frying.

Fill two-thirds of the cone first then push the filling down with a spoon and add more filling. Now close the opening by pinching and folding the two edges together to form a pleated top.

Line a colander with kitchen roll to absorb excess ghee.

Fill a karhai / wok or deep-frying pan three quarters full with ghee and heat over a medium flame.

When the ghee is hot enough, fry the samosas a few at a time.

Fry for approximately 10 minutes turning the samosas over with a slotted spoon often, until both sides are golden brown. Remove and drain into the lined colander.

Alternative fillings which can used are diced potatoes, peppers and minced paneer, or peas and minced paneer. See 3.2 for paneer preparation.

Serve with one of these chutneys: cooked or fresh tomatoes chutney, fruit, tamarind, or avocado chutney.

N.B. Instead of using the selection of spices described above, an alternative option is to add ghee (50 ml) to a large non-stick wok over a medium heat followed by punch pooran (3 tbs), chopped green chillies (2), grated ginger (2 tbs) and the mixed vegetables followed by asafetida (1 tsp), turmeric (1 tsp) and salt (1 ½ tsp). Mix and cook for 15 minutes, cool the filling, spoon into the prepared cones and deep-fry as described above.

Preparation time: 20 min   Cooking and frying time: 60 min

Ingredients

3 ½ litres full fat milk
300 ml bottled lemon juice
2 red peppers or
1 courgette and 1 green pepper

50 ml olive oil
2 ½ tbs ginger
2 chopped green chillies
1 ½ tsp asafetida
1 tsp kalonji seeds
1 tsp salt
¾ tsp black pepper
1 tsp turmeric
1 tsp paprika powder

Pastry for 16 samosas
2 cups self raising flour
1 ½ cups plain flour
1 ½ tsp salt
1 ½ tsp kalonji seeds
8 tbs or ½ cup melted ghee
1 cup hot water

Preparation Method

Paneer is made as described in recipe 3.2 from full fat milk (3 ½ litres) and bottled lemon juice (300 ml).

Press the prepared paneer for not more than fifteen minutes using a heavy weight which could be the same pot used to make the paneer filled with water.

Wash and cut red peppers (2) into half, remove the seeds and dice into 1 cm cubes.

Alternatively choose courgette (1) and green pepper (1), wash, cut, remove the seeds of the green pepper and dice into pieces no more than (1 cm) cubed.

In a large stainless steel mixing bowl make the pastry from self raising flour (2 cups), plain flour (1 ½ cups), salt (1 ½ tsp), melted ghee (½ cup), kalonji seeds (1 ½ tsp) and hot water (1 cup).

Mix by hand for 5 minutes until the dough is soft and smooth. Empty the dough onto the work top and continue kneading by pushing back and forth with both hands. Cover with the mixing bowl and allow to rest.

Add olive oil (1 ladle not more than 50 ml) to a non stick medium sized wok, over a medium flame. Throw in crushed ginger (2 ½ tbs), chopped green chillies (1-2), asafetida (1-1 ½ tsp), kalonji seeds (1 tsp).

Stir fry for 1-2 minutes and add either the diced red peppers or the diced courgette and green pepper.

Cook for 10 minutes add salt (1 tsp), black pepper (¾ tsp), turmeric (1 tsp) and paprika powder (1 tsp).

When these vegetables are almost cooked add the crumbly paneer, mix and continue cooking for a further 5 minutes. Transfer the filling to a medium sized baking tray and spread evenly and allow to cool to room temperature. When cool, divide into 16 equal portions see recipe 6.3 which describes how to do this.

Take a large stainless steel baking tray either smear the surface with sunflower oil or cover the base with baking paper.

Return to the pastry, continue kneading and shape into a long French roll (30-35 cm) long and divide equally into 16 pieces see chapati recipe 5.1.

Each piece is made into a small ball rounded in between the palms of your hands flattened and then rolled out to give a circle approximately 15 cm in diameter.

Using a tablespoon fill the centre with the paneer vegetable mix and shape the filling similar into a heaped small mountain.

Bring the ends together, seal and flute to give the first pastry samosa. Similar to a half moon shape. Repeat this procedure until all 16 pastry samosas have been prepared.

Carefully position the samosas on the tray pierce the tops with a fork or a knife.

Glaze with sour cream or yogurt using a small brush and bake in a **preheated oven** at 180°C for 30-40 minutes. When golden brown remove the tray from the oven.

Transfer to small plates and serve with cooked or fresh tomato chutney, fruit, tamarind or avocado chutney.

Preparation and cooking time: 40 min   Baking time: 30-40 min

Ingredients

1 cup sieved chickpea flour
1 ½ cup plain yogurt
1 ½ cup water
2 tbs finely grated ginger
2 finely chopped green chillies
1 ½ tsp salt
1 tsp turmeric

Masala for topping
45 ml ghee
1 tsp mustard seeds
2 tbs sesame seeds
dessicated coconut for sprinkling
sprinkle paprika powder
¼ bunch chopped
coriander leaves

Preparation Method

Sieve chickpea flour (1 cup) into a large cooking pot.

Next add plain yogurt (1 ½ cups), water (1 ½ cups), followed by finely grated ginger (2 tbs) and finely chopped green chillies (2), salt (1 ½ tsp) and turmeric (1 tsp).

Place the pot over a medium flame. Mix first by whisking briskly and when a consistent mixture is observed change to a wooden square spoon so that during the mixing any mixture which sticks to the sides are gathered and returned to the centre maintaining a uniform cooking. This vigorous mixing and gathering from the sides prevents burning.

Cook for 15 minutes mixing continuously.

To confirm the khandvi is cooked hit the sides of the pot with the wooden spoon, if the khandvi easily drops back into the pot it is ready. Do not overcook the khandvi.

After cooking transfer the khandvi either onto a clean and dry stainless steel kitchen surface or a large steel tray or a marble kitchen work surface.

Immediately spread the cooked khandvi as thinly as possible with the largest plastic spatula available covering the entire table 1 ½ metre x 40 cm.

Leave the spreaded khandvi on the table for a minimum of 15 minutes to set and cool. Cut horizontally in half first and each half is cut across into smaller strips 2-3 cm in width.

Roll each strip tightly using fingers and thumbs into small Swiss rolls shapes and transfer to small plates.

Add a simple topping made from heating ghee (45 ml) with a mixture of popped mustard seeds (1 tsp) and sesame seeds (2 tbs). Cook for 1-2 minutes over a medium flame and pour evenly over the prepared khandvi, sprinkle with dessicated coconut, paprika powder, finely chopped coriander leaves (¼ bunch) and serve with coriander chutney.

Cooking time: 15 min   Preparation time: 15 min

Ingredients

3 cups chickpea flour
850 ml water
550 ml yogurt

3-4 chopped green chillies
3 tbs grated ginger
2 tsp salt
½ tsp turmeric
¼ bunch chopped
coriander leaves or 12-14 curry leaves

Preparation Method

Grease a medium sized baking tray with oil and set aside.
Mix chickpea flour (3 cups) with water (850 ml), yogurt (550 ml), salt (2 tsp), turmeric (½ tsp), chopped chillies (3-4) and grated ginger (3 tbs) in a medium sized pot over a medium flame.

Cook by whisking briskly first and when a consistent mixture is obtained change to a wooden square spoon and follow the procedure as described in the recipe for khandvi 6.5.

Cook for 15 minutes, and when the vada is almost cooked (no visible lumps leaving a smooth texture) add washed, freshly chopped coriander leaves (¼ bunch).
Instead of coriander stir 12-14 curry leaves in heated ghee (35 ml) for 1-2 minutes and then add the leaves to the vada continue mixing and cook for a further 2-5 minutes.

Using a medium sized plastic spatula transfer the cooked vada into standard baking tray as quickly as possible since the mixture will want to set in the pot.

Spread evenly into the corners using a plastic spatula.

Wet your hands with cold water and gently press down and level the top several times.

Cool to room temperature which should take about 30-40 minutes.

Cut along the sides of the baking tray and turn the tray upside down. The cooked vada should fall out intact.

The rectangular vada is cut into diamond shapes by first cutting the entire rectangular block lengthwise into approximately 3 cm widths and then cut diagonally across into diamond shapes starting from top left corner working across to the bottom about 7 cm spacing between each cut.

Line a colander with kitchen roll to absorb excess ghee.

Deep-fry these daimond shaped vadas in a karhai / wok or deep-frying pan three quarters full with ghee over a medium flame adding 10 diamond shaped vadas at a time. Turn regularly with a slotted spoon for consistent cooking. Remove vadas after 5-10 minutes frying.

Transfer the fried vadas to the lined colander and then place on plates with one of these chutneys: fresh coriander chutney, cooked or fresh tomato chutney or avocado chutney and serve.

Preparation time: 5 min   Cooking time: 15 min   Frying time: 15-20 min

Ingredients

1 ½ cups medium semolina
2 tbs chickpea flour
¼ cup oil
2 finely chopped green chillies
1 tbs grated ginger
1 ¼ tsp salt
½ tsp turmeric
1 tsp sugar
1 ½ cups yogurt
2 tbs lemon juice
1-2 tbs water
2 tsp ENO

Topping for Dokra
35 ml ghee
1 tsp mustard seeds
2 tbs sesame seeds
1 tsp paprika powder
2 tsp desiccated coconut
¼ bunch chopped
coriander leaves

Preparation Method

To a large mixing bowl add semolina (1 ½ cup), chickpea flour (2 tbs), oil (¼ cup), followed by finely chopped green chillies (2), fresh grated ginger (1 tbs), salt (1 ¼ tsp), turmeric (½ tsp) and sugar (1 tsp). Mix by whisking breaking up any visible lumps.

Next add yogurt (1 ½ cups), lemon juice (2 tbs), water (1-2 tbs), ENO (2 tsp) and whisk.

The dokra mix is now ready for steam cooking.

In a large pot or mixing bowl 40 cm in diameter fill with water about 5 cm deep and bring to the boil over a medium to high flame.

Place a metal ring approximately 15 cm in diameter and height (2-3 cm) inside the pot.

Transfer the dokra mixture to either a round cake tin 25 cm in diameter or a square cake tin of similar diameter and spread evenly.

Position the filled cake tin on top of the ring, tightly fit a lid and steam cook for 20 minutes.

More water can be added along the side of the bowl or pot to maintain the steaming.

Treat the dokra like a cake. Insert a knife into the centre of the dokra and remove if the knife is dry the dokra is cooked.

Using metal tongs remove the cake tin carefully and allow to rest on a cooling tray.

In a smaller pot over a medium flame the topping is made by heating ghee (small ladle 35 ml), with mustard seeds (1 tsp). After the seeds have popped add sesame seeds (2 tbs) cook for 1-2 minutes pour the hot mixture on the dokra and spread evenly, garnish with paprika powder (1 tsp), desiccated coconut (2 tsp) and washed, freshly chopped coriander leaves (¼ bunch).

Cut the dokra around the edges first then cut the from the centre into equal portions, remove and serve with fresh coriander chutney. See ondwa 6.8 on how to cut into 16 equal pieces.

Preparation time: 10 min   Cooking time: 20 min

Ingredients

2 cups ondwa flour
¼ cup coarse semolina
¾-1 cup yogurt
1 cup hot water
1 lauki / dudhi
2 carrots
½ cup frozen peas
200 g cabbage (optional)

2 tbs oil
2 tsp salt
2 tsp sugar
½ tsp turmeric
2 tbs grated ginger
2 chopped green chillies
1 tsp ENO
¼ cup sesame seeds

Preparation Method

(Ondwa flour, obtained from Indian grocery shops, is a mixture of chickpea flour or finely ground chana dal, rice and turmeric powder.)

Wash, peel and grate one lauki / dudhi through the large holes of a grater, into a large mixing bowl.

To the grated lauki add ondwa flour (2 cups), followed by yogurt (¾-1 cup), semolina (¼ cup), hot water (1 cup), oil (2 tbs), salt (2 tsp), sugar (2 tsp), turmeric (½ tsp), grated ginger (2 tbs), chopped green chillies (3) and ENO (1 tsp).

Next add washed, peeled and grated carrots (2). Add frozen peas (1 cup) to a sieve wash with hot water and add it to the mixture.

Washed and grated cabbage (200 g) is an additional extra.

Mix throughly with a stainless spoon.

Cover the base of a baking tray with greaseproof paper and then transfer the mixture from the mixing bowl into the baking tray, spread evenly, and liberally cover the top with sesame seeds (¼ cup) and bake in a **preheated oven** at 190°C for 40-60 minutes.

Check the ondwa is cooked by inserting a knife into the middle of the ondwa. If the knife is dry the ondwa is cooked.

Cool to room temperature, cut along the edges first and then cut into 16 pieces, remove carefully. Place four pieces per small tray and serve with either fresh coriander chutney or cooked or fresh tomato chutney.

N.B. To get 16 equal portions cut a cross through the ondwa to give 4 equal quarters. Next cut two straight lines either side of the vertical centre line and two more lines either side of the horizontal centre line. This will give 16 equal portions. Lift the square pieces carefully transfer to small plates and serve.

Preparation time: 10 min   Baking time approximately: 60 min

6.9 Alu patra (potatoes in pastry)

Ingredients

5-6 red potatoes approx 1 kg

2 tsp ghee
1 tsp mustard seeds
½ tsp asafetida
1 tsp salt
1 tsp sugar
1 tsp sesame seeds
¼ tsp black pepper
¼ cup bottled lemon juice
⅓ tsp cinnamon powder
¼ tsp cloves powder
3 tbs desiccated coconut
2 tbs grated ginger
2 chopped green chillies
¼ cup potato starch / farina
⅓ bunch chopped
coriander leaves

Dough for frying

2 cups plain flour
1 cup chickpea flour
¼ cup yogurt
1 cup hot water
1 tbs oil
1 tsp salt

Dough for baked alu patra

3 cups self raising flour
½ cup melted ghee
1 ½ tsp salt
1 cup warm water (approximately)

Preparation Method (for frying)

Wash red potatoes (5-6, 1 kg) and add them to a large pot of water. Bring the water to the boil over a medium flame and continue boiling until the potatoes are soft.

Pierce one of the potatoes with a knife to check if they are cooked.

Remove the pot from the heat and drain the water. Take care during the draining process.

Allow the potatoes to cool to room temperature.

To a large mixing bowl add plain flour (2 cups), followed by chickpea flour (1 cup), salt (1 tsp), oil (1 tbs), yogurt (¼ cup), hot water (1 cup).

Mix by hand to make a dough. Remove the dough place it on the work surface, cover it with a tea-towel and set aside to rest.

Return to the cooled potatoes, remove the skin and mash. If the mashed potatoes are watery add some potato starch also known as farina and mix.

In a smaller pot over a medium flame make a mixture of spices (chaunce) with ghee (2 tsp), popped mustard seeds (1 tsp), asafetida (½ tsp). Mix and add the spice mixture to the mashed potatoes followed by salt (1 tsp), sugar (1 tsp), sesame seeds (1 tsp), black pepper (¼ tsp), bottled lemon juice (¼ cup), cinnamon powder (⅓ tsp), cloves powder (¼ tsp), desiccated coconut (3 tbs), grated ginger (2 tbs), chopped green chillies (2), washed and chopped coriander leaves (⅓ bunch).

Mix by hand and allow to stand. If the potatoes appear to be wet add potato starch / farina (¼ cup approximately) and continue to mix.

Return to the dough, flour the rolling surface liberally, roll out the entire dough into a rectangle 30 cm in length 40-50 cm width with a thickness of about (4 mm).

Spread the cooled mashed potato mixture evenly on the rolled pastry surface. Cover your hands with flour to prevent them from sticking to the dough and roll the pastry to make a tight, compact, large Swiss roll.

Using a sharp serrated knife cut the rolled potato filled pastry into 1.5 cm slices. Reshape into rounds and place on a platter ready for frying.

Line a flat topped colander with kitchen roll to absorb excess ghee.

Deep-fry the alu patra in a karhai / wok or deep-frying pan three quarters full with ghee, over a high flame.

The ghee is hot enough for frying when a pinch of dough dropped into the ghee rises immediately to the surface and sizzles.

Place several slices into the hot ghee and fry them for 3-5 min, turning them gently over with a slotted spoon once until they are golden-brown.

When all the alu patras have been fried remove with a slotted spoon drain the excess ghee and transfer to the lined colander.

Add several to small plates and serve with one of these chutneys: fresh coriander and coconut chutney, fresh tomato chutney, tamarind or avocado chutney.

Boiling time: 20 min   Preparation time: 20 min   Frying time: 15 min

N.B. Alu patras can also be baked. For baking use self raising flour (3 cups) and continue to prepare the alu patras as described above, then cut and place the slices on a tray and bake in a **preheated oven** at 180°C until golden brown, which should take between 25-30 minutes. Remove and glaze the tops with butter. Transfer to a plate and serve with tamarind or plum chutney.

6.10 PATRA

Ingredients

1 large packet of patra leaves
45 ml ghee
1 tbs mustard seeds
3 tbs sesame seeds

3 cups chickpea flour
4 tsp salt
1 tbs grated ginger
1 tsp chilli powder
2 tbs grated jaggery
3 tbs oil
2 tbs tamarind or ¾ cup bottled lemon juice
1 cup hot water approx
3 tbs sesame seeds

Preparation Method

Unwrap patra leaves, there should be at least 20 medium sized individual leaves.

Wash the leaves first and with a knife cut and remove the Y shaped stem which holds the leaves together. This stem is hard and must be removed.

To a mixing bowl make the paste with chickpea flour (3 cups), salt (4 tsp), grated ginger (1 tbs), chilli powder (1 tsp), grated jaggery (2 tbs), oil (3 tbs), tamarind (2 tbs) or bottled lemon juice (¾ cup) *not both*, followed by sesame seeds (3 tbs) and hot water (approximately 1 cup). Mix to give a thick paste.

Turn the leaves over and spread the thick paste on the dull side with a plastic spatula and place one leaf one on top of each other in opposite directions.

Fold each pair similar to closing a letter envelope. Turn them over and add more batter to seal the leaves tightly. Roll one end up and continue rolling to make shapes similar to Swiss rolls.

Half fill the largest wok available with water and heat over a high flame.

Place a circular cooling tray in the centre of the wok above the water. During the steam cooking add more water if needed along the side of the wok.

Add all the rolled patra on the top of the cooling tray and steam cook for 40 minutes.

Turn the heat off and let the steamed patras cool.

Remove the steamed patras carefully from the cooling tray. Cut each rolled patra on a cutting board into as many (1-1.5 cm) slices.

Place the sliced patras on flat plates garnish with a heated mixture of mustard seeds (1 tbs), in ghee (1 small ladle full 45 ml), sesame seeds (3 tbs) and serve with cooked or fresh tomato chutney or tamarind chutney.

N.B. Alternatively sliced patras can also be deep-fried in a karhai / wok or deep-frying pan three quarters filled with ghee and heated over a high flame. Remove the fried patras with a slotted spoon, drain and set aside in a colander lined with a kitchen roll to absorb excess ghee. Transfer to plates, ganish as described above and serve with the mentioned chutneys.

Preparation time: 20 min   Steam cooking time: 25 min   Frying time: 10 min

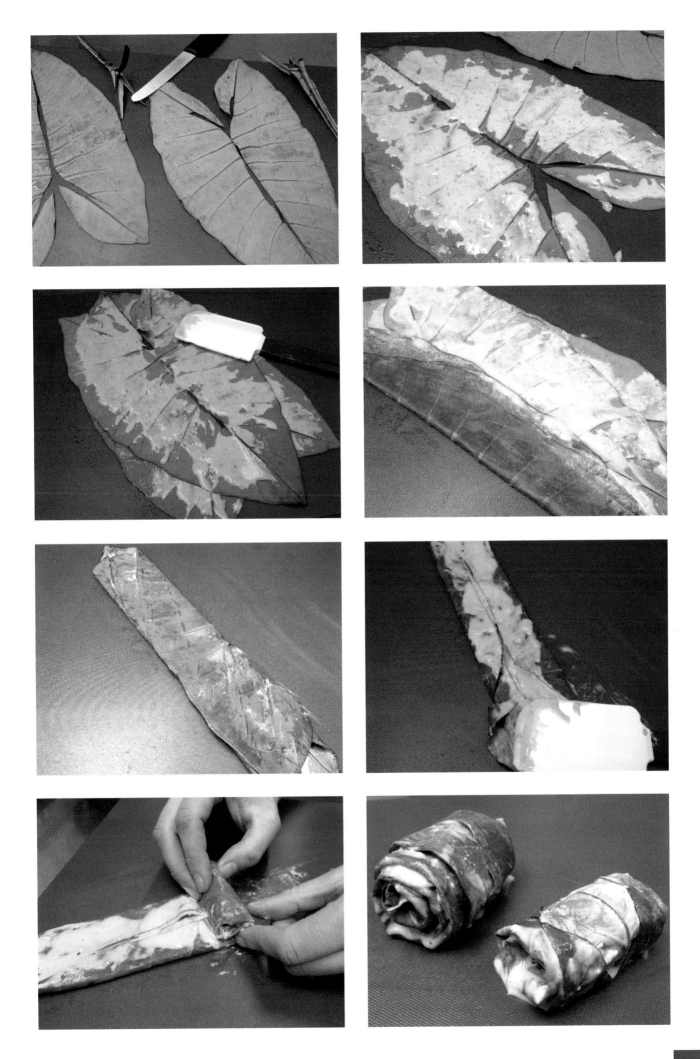

6.11 PUDLA

Ingredients

5 cups chickpea flour
1 large or 2 small tomatoes
½ cup peas
1 finely chopped red pepper
½ bunch coriander
3 cups warm water approx

2 tsp salt
2 tbs grated ginger
3 chopped green chillies
1 tsp paprika powder
1 ½ tsp ENO powder

Preparation Method

Pudla is a flat savoury pancake made from chickpea flour.

To a large mixing bowl add chickpea flour (5 cups), salt (2 tsp), finely chopped chillies (3), grated ginger (3 tbs) and paprika powder (1 tsp).

Next add finely chopped tomatoes (1 big or 2 small), followed by the addition of defrosted peas (½ cup), finely chopped red peppers (1), washed and finely chopped fresh coriander leaves (½ bunch), ENO (1 ½ tsp) and mix.

Now add warm water (approximately 3 cups), stirring continuously until a medium thick pancake batter is obtained.

Take two medium sized frying pans or (2 tavas) and under a low flame add ghee to cover the hot plate.

A medium sized ladle is half filled with the batter and then the batter is poured from the ladle onto the hot plate.

With the underside of the ladle press the heap of batter flat and turn left to right evenly spreading the batter into a pancake shape 14 cm in diameter.

Cook slowly on both sides until golden brown, add a further teaspoon of ghee and cover with a suitable sized lid leave to cook for 4-5 minutes on each side.

After cooking stack 8 pudlas 14 cm in diameter on a cutting board and carefully cut the pile in half to give 16 pieces and serve with fresh tomato chutney.

Preparation time: 15 min   Cooking time: 30 min

6.12 Pea kachori

Ingredients

3 ½ cups frozen peas
1 carrot or mashed paneer 1 cup

45 ml ghee
1 tsp mustard seeds
2 tbs grated ginger
2 green chillies
½ tsp asafetida
1 tsp turmeric
1 ½ tsp garam masala
1 tsp sugar
1 tsp salt

Dough for 16 kachoris
3 cups plain flour
1 cup water
1 cup oil
1 tsp salt
1 tsp lemon juice

Preparation Method

Frozen peas (3 ½ cups) are added to a sieve and defrosted by washing with hot water. Transfer to a food blender partially blend for a few seconds by pulsing several times and keep in the blender until needed.

One medium sized carrot is washed peeled and grated through the large holes of a stainless steel grater.

Make the masala in a non-stick pan over a medium heat. First add ghee (1 ladle 45 ml), toss in mustard seeds (1 tsp) and let the seeds pop, then add grated ginger (2 tbs), chopped green chillies (2), asafetida (½ tsp) and mix.

Now introduce the partially blended peas and the grated carrots or in place of the carrots mashed paneer (1 cup). See paneer preparation 3.2. Use full fat milk (1 litre) and bottled lemon juice (85 ml). Next add turmeric (1 tsp), garam masala (1 ½ tsp), sugar (1 tsp) and salt (1 tsp).

Cook for 10 minutes remove the pan from heat and cool to room temperature.

Use an electric blender to mix water (1 cup), oil (1 cup) and lemon juice (1 tsp) for 1-2 minutes or until the mixture is milky in colour. Pour the mixture to plain flour (3 cups) in a large mixing bowl add salt (1 tsp) and make the dough.

Mix and knead to give a flexible dough and let it rest for 10 minutes covered.

Shape the dough into an elongated French stick (30-35 cm) long and divide into 16 equal pieces like chapati preparation see 5.1.

Roll each piece into circles (8-10 cm) in diameter.

Using a tablespoon add the cooked kachori mixture into the centre of the rolled pastry.

Lift and join the ends of the rolled pastry above the fillings. Twist the top of the combined ends sealing the contents. Discard surplus twisted pastry or add it to the next portion of pastry.

Flatten or leave as a ball. This is an individual preference.

Line a colander with kitchen roll to absorb excess ghee. Set up a karhai / wok or deep-frying pan over a medium flame, three quarters filled with ghee.

Deep-fry the kachoris until golden brown, remove with a slotted spoon, drain and transfer to the lined colander.

Place on small plates and serve with one of these chutneys, fresh coriander chutney or cooked tomato chutney.

Preparation time: 25 min   Cooking time: 10 min   Frying time: 20 min

6.13 LAUKI / DUDHI KOFTA

Ingredients

1 large or 2 small sized lauki
1 ½ cup chickpea flour
½ cup rice flour

1 ½ tsp salt
2 green chillies
2 tbs grated ginger
1 tsp whole coriander seeds
1 tsp asafetida
1 tsp turmeric
2 tbs lemon juice
½ tsp sugar
½ tsp ENO
⅓ bunch chopped
coriander leaves

Preparation Method

Choose lauki / dudhi (1 large or 2 small).

Wash, peel and grate the lauki through the large holes of the grater into a mixing bowl.

To the grated lauki add chickpea flour (1 ½ cups) and rice flour (½ cup). Mix with salt (1 ½ tsp), finely chopped green chillies, grated ginger (2 tbs), whole coriander seeds (1 tsp), asafetida (1 tsp), turmeric (1 tsp), lemon juice (2 tbs), sugar (½ tsp), ENO (½ tsp) washed and finely chopped coriander leaves (⅓ bunch).

Mix without any further addition of water to give a yellow mixture.

Line a colander with kitchen roll to absorb excess ghee.

Set up a karhai / wok or deep-frying pan three quarters filled with ghee and heat over a medium flame.

Using fingers and thumb of the right or left hand, make ball shapes from the batter and carefully place about fifteen ball shaped koftas into the hot ghee.

Deep-fry for 10 minutes or when the koftas are golden brown remove the koftas with a slotted spoon drain and transfer to the lined colander.

Repeat the process with the remaining half of the batter.

Place on trays and serve with one of these chutneys fresh coriander chutney, cooked or fresh tomato chutney or tamarind chutney.

N.B. If lauki is not available use grated cabbage (1 medium sized), grated carrot (1 medium sized) and ½ cup of frozen peas. Mix with chickpea flour (1 ½ cups) and all the mentioned spices, make balls and fry in the same manner and serve with the same chutneys mentioned.

Preparation time: 20 min   Frying time: 20 min

Ingredients

2 cups basmati rice
1 cup urad dal
water

1 chopped green chilli
1 tbs grated ginger

Preparation Method

The above quantities will make (approximately 35 steamed rice spongy savoury cakes) called idlis.

To a medium sized bowl add a mixture of basmati rice (2 cups) and urad dal (1 cup). Add warm water and soak either overnight or a minimum 6-8 hours.

Drain the water using a colander and the collected rice and dal are transferred to a food processor and blended for 2 minutes. Use a small amount water to give a slurry.

Then transfer the blended mixture to an electric blender and continue blending for 5 minutes to give a very fine smooth batter.

Transfer it back to a clean bowl and allow to stand overnight in a warm place to allow the fermentation process to continue.

The next morning if fermentation has not occurred add ENO (1 ½ tsp) and after effervescence add salt (1 tsp), finely chopped green chilli (1) and grated ginger (1 tbs). Mix and prepare for steam cooking.

Assemble 4 stainless steel stacked trays 15 cm in diameter where each individual tray has a 3 cup shaped indentations for the idli mixture.

Grease each cup cake shaped indentation with ghee / oil and fill each one three quarters full with the idli mixture and place the stack of trays on a ring immersed in 10 cm of water inside a larger pot over a medium flame.

Steam cook for 10 minutes. Add extra water along the side of the pot to maintain steaming.

Check to see if the idlis are cooked by piercing the centre with a small knife. If the knife edge is dry the idli is cooked, if the edge is wet continue steaming.

Remove the cooked idlis gently using a stainless steel spoon to give the first batch of flying saucer shaped idlis.

Brush the insides of the cup-cake shaped indentations again with more ghee / oil.

Add more water to the pot to create the steam cooking atmosphere again.

Spoon in the remaining idli mixture and continue steam cooking. In this way complete the cooking process until all the batter has been used up.

Place on serving plates with fresh coriander or fresh coconut yogurt chutney.

Soaking time: 6-8 hrs followed by 2 nights standing overnight

Preparation time: 20 min   Steaming time: 20 min

6.15 Dahivada

Ingredients

⅓ cup split mung dal
1 cup urad dal
1 tbs grated ginger
1 chopped green chilli
1 tsp salt
⅓ tsp bicarbonate soda

4-5 cups yogurt
1 tsp sugar
½ tsp salt
1 ½ tsp cumin seeds
½ tsp paprika powder
¼ bunch fresh coriander leaves

Preparation Method

Mix split mung dal (⅓ cup) and urad dal (1 cup). Soak in a bowl of water for 4 hours.

Decant the water and blend the mixture of dals in a food processor. Add water if needed.

Transfer the blended dals to a mixing bowl, add grated ginger (1 tbs), salt (1 tsp), crushed green chilli (1) and bicarbonate of soda (⅓ tsp).

Fill a karhai / wok or deep-frying pan three quarters with ghee and heat over a medium flame.

Using the first three fingers and the thumb of the left or right hand take the mixed dal mixture from the bowl shape into balls and push the runny dal into the hot ghee.

Deep-fry until golden brown in colour.

Remove the fried vadas from the ghee with a slotted spoon drain excess ghee and soak in a bowl of salted warm water [salt (½ tsp) and water (3 litres)] for 30 minutes.

Squeeze the water out gently by pressing the vadas between your palms and place several vadas on flat plates.

Next roast cumin seeds (1 ½ tsp) on a tava or hot plate over a medium flame.

Transfer the roasted cumin seeds to a pestle and mortar and grind or place the roasted cumin seeds on the clean kitchen worktop and run a rolling pin over the seeds several times.

Thoroughly mix yogurt (4-5 cups) with sugar (1 tsp), salt (½ tsp), in a jug and pour the yogurt mixture on top of fried vadas.

Garnish with the roasted cumin seeds, paprika powder (½ tsp) and finely chopped coriander leaves (¼ bunch) and serve with tamarind chutney.

N.B. Small amounts of tamarind chutney can be added on the top of the vadas.

Preparation time: 4 hours or overnight soaking

Soaking in salty water: 30 min   Frying time: 15 min

6.16 SPINACH AND PANEER PIE

Ingredients

800 g spinach
2 litres full fat milk
160 ml bottled lemon juice
½-1 cup soured cream

30-45 ml olive oil
1 tbs grated ginger
1 chopped green chilli
1 tsp asafetida
3 tbs Italian herbs
1 tsp black pepper
1 tsp salt

Pastry
1 ½ cups of plain flour
1 ½ cups of self raising flour
230 g butter
1 ½ tsp salt
½ cup plain yogurt

Preparation Method

First prepare paneer as described in recipe 3.2 using full fat milk (2 litres) and bottled lemon juice (170 ml). Keep the pressing to a minimum.

To a large mixing bowl add plain flour (1 ½ cups), self raising flour (1 ½ cups), sliced butter (230 g) and salt (1 ½ tsp). Lightly rub the butter with the fingertips until the flour and butter mixture looks like fine breadcrumbs. Next add yogurt (½ cup) and continue to knead to give the pastry.

Divide the pastry into two portions. Grease a large baking tray and roll out one portion of pastry to cover the base. Pierce the base with a fork. Trim the edges and bake the base in a **preheated oven** at 160°C for 15-20 minutes or until golden.

During this baking period take a large pot and add olive oil (1 small ladle 30 / 45 ml), followed by grated ginger (1 tbs), chopped green chilli (1), asafetida (1 tsp), washed and chopped spinach (800 g or one full colander).

Cook for ten minutes first, then add Italian herbs (3 tbs), ground black pepper (1 tsp) and salt (1 tsp) followed by the prepared paneer.

Next add soured cream (½-1 cup) and mix. Reserve a small amount for brushing the top.

Add the cooked spinach on top of the baked base pastry and spread evenly.

Roll out the second half of the pastry and cover the filling. Brush the top with soured cream or yogurt, pierce top with a fork and bake in the oven at 160°C for 20 minutes.

Remove from the oven and allow to cool. Cut into 16 equal portions see recipe for ondwa 6.6. Remove the slices carefully and serve.

Preparation time: 20 min   Baking time: 45 min

6.17 STUFFED TOMATO WITH RICE

Ingredients

¾ cup rice
1 ½ cups water
1 small chopped red pepper
hand full cashew nuts
½ cup frozen peas
16 tomatoes

45 ml ghee
1 tsp salt
½ tsp turmeric
¼ tsp black pepper
1 tsp Italian herbs

Preparation Method

Cook fancy rice as described in 2.1 and set aside.

Choose 16 medium sized tomatoes. Slice off the top third of the tomatoes and reserve, (this will serve as the 'lid' for the stuffed tomatoes).

Gently scoop out the pulp carefully using a tablespoon to cut around the edges. Keep the pulp of the tomatoes for chutney.

At this stage you should have 16 tomato shells on cup cake trays. Transfer the cooked rice to a baking tray and divide into 16 equal portions, see recipe 6.3 which describes how to do this.

Fill the empty tomato shells with the cooked fancy rice using a tablespoon. Replace the tops of the tomatoes and bake in a **preheated oven** at 150°C for 10-15 minutes.

Remove from the oven allow to cool then transfer to serving plates accompanied with green chutney.

Optional vegetables for fancy rice are: chopped spinach (1 bunch) and a medium sized courgette (1).

Preparation time: 20 min   Baking time: 10-15 min

N.B. Alternatively stuff red peppers with the same filling.

Take red peppers (8) wash and cut each into half and remove the seeds. Fill with the above prepared rice and bake in a **pre-heated oven** at 150°C for 10-15 minutes. Cool and serve with yogurt and cashew nut chutney.

CHUTNEYS

Ingredients

1 medium sized fresh coriander
1 cup yogurt
¾ cup desiccated coconut
1-2 tsp lemon juice

1 tbs grated ginger
2 tbs chopped green chillies
¾ tsp salt
1 tsp sugar

Preparation Method

Wash a medium sized fresh coriander to remove dirt from the leaves and stems. Cut the bunch into smaller pieces starting from the top down to the root ends. Do not include the root ends discard about (4-6 cm) from the end.

Add to an electric blender yogurt (1 cup), followed by chopped pieces of the fresh coriander, then salt (¾ tsp), sugar (1 tsp), lemon juice (1-2 tsp), green chillies (2), grated ginger (1 tbs) and desiccated coconut (¾ cup).

Blend transfer to small bowls and serve with a savoury.

Preparation time: 5-10 min

Ingredients

3 tomatoes
1 red pepper
1 tsp lemon juice
⅓ cup raw peanuts (optional)

½ tsp salt
¾ tsp sugar
1 tbs grated ginger
1-2 green chillies

Preparation Method

Take one red pepper, cut into slices and add to an electric blender. Next take tomatoes (3), cut into cubes and add to the blender, followed by lemon juice (1 tsp), raw peanuts (optional ⅓ cup), salt (½ tsp), sugar (¾ tsp), grated ginger (1 tbs) and green chillies (1-2), mix until liquid, transfer to bowls and serve with a savoury.

Preparation time: 5 min

Ingredients

5-6 medium sized blended tomatoes

45 ml ghee
2 cinnamon sticks
5 dry chillies
1 ½ tsp whole cumin seeds
2 tbs jaggery or 2 tbs sugar
¾ tsp salt
¼ cup raisins

Preparation Method

Wash and blend tomatoes (5-6).

Add ghee (1 ladle 45 ml) to a medium sized pot and heat over a medium flame. Next add cinnamon sticks (2), dry chillies (5) and whole cumin seeds (1 ½ tsp).

Cook for 1 minute and add the washed and blended tomatoes followed by jaggery (2 tbs) or sugar (2 tbs), salt (¾ tsp), raisins (¼ cup) and cook for 10-15 minutes.

Transfer to bowls and serve with a savoury.

Preparation time: 5 min   Cooking time: 15 min

Ingredients

6 medium sized tomatoes
10-12 dates

45 ml ghee
1 tbs punch pooran
2 bay leaves
3 dry red chillies
¾ tsp salt
2 tbs jaggery or brown sugar

Preparation Method

In a large pot boil water (½ litre). When the water comes to the boil add the tomatoes (6) and keep them in the boling water for 2-3 minutes. Remove the pot from the heat.

Drain, blanch the tomatoes and slice into equal pieces.

Wash dates (10-12) in a sieve and remove the seeds.

In a small cooking pot, over a medium flame, add ghee (1 ladle 45 ml). Next add punch pooran (1 tbs), bay leaves (2), large dry red chillies (2), followed by the addition of the blanched tomato pieces, dates, salt (¾ tsp), jaggery or brown sugar (2 tbs).

Mix and cook for 10 minutes.

Remove from the heat and serve in small bowls with a savoury.

Preparation time: 10 min   Cooking time: 10 min

7.5 Avocado

Ingredients

1 large or 2 medium sized avocados
¾-1 cup yogurt
¾ cup cashew nuts either baked
roasted or deep-fried

½ tsp asafetida
1 tbs honey
¼ tsp black pepper
½ tsp salt
1 green chilli
2 tbs grated ginger

Preparation Method

If using baked cashew nuts, bake the cashew nuts (¾ cup) in a **preheated oven** at 170°C for 5 minutes first.

or

Deep-fry the cashew nuts in a karhai / wok or deep-frying pan filled three quarters with ghee heated over a medium flame. Remove when brown in colour with a slotted spoon drain and set aside in a colander lined with kitchen roll.

or

Roast the cashew nuts on a tava over a medium flame until brown in colour and remove from the heat.

Chose a medium to soft avocado (1 large or 2 medium sized), wash and peel. Cut into half and remove the stone.

To an electric blender add plain yogurt (¾ -1 cup) first, then add either roasted, fried or baked cashew nuts, the peeled avocado pair, black pepper (¼ tsp), salt (½ tsp), asafetida (½ tsp), honey (1 tbs), green chilli (1) and grated ginger (2 tbs) and mix to give a smooth paste.

Transfer to serving bowls and serve with a savoury.

Preparation time: 10 min

Avocados

7.6 Fruit chutney (apple)

Ingredients

5-6 medium sized apples

30 ml ghee
1 cinnamon stick
1 tsp cumin seeds
4-5 whole cloves
½ tsp asafetida
¾ tsp turmeric
⅓ tsp chilli powder
½ cup sugar

Preparation Method

Wash and peel apples (5-6 medium sized), remove the core and seeds and cut into cubes.

Add ghee (1 small ladle 30 ml) to a small pot, over a medium flame. Next add cinnamon stick (1), cumin seeds (1 tsp), whole cloves (4-5), asafetida (½ tsp) and turmeric (¾ tsp).

Introduce the cubed apple, chilli powder (⅓ tsp) and finally sugar (½ cup). Cook for 15 minutes, remove from the heat, transfer to bowls and serve with a savoury.

The following fruits can also be used: pears, peaches, pineapple, mango, nectarines and plums.

With peaches, plums, and nectarines there is no need to remove the skin. Wash, cut, remove the stones and slice into equal sized pieces or cut into cubes and cook as above.

Preparation time: 10 min   Cooking time: 15 min

Use red plums (600 g) and follow the method above to make plum chutney.

Ingredients

1 brown coconut

1 ½ cups plain yogurt

¾ tsp salt

1 tsp sugar

10 fresh coriander leaves

45 ml ghee

2 tsp urad dal

1 tsp fenugreek

10 curry leaves

½ tsp asafetida

2 tbs grated ginger

2 chopped green chillies

Preparation Method

Take a whole coconut and break the shell by either tapping the middle firmly with the blunt side of a large knife or hitting gently with a hammer so that the coconut splits into two halves.

Filter the coconut water through a sieve into a liquid blender. The pulp can be removed from the shell either by heating the shells directly over a hot flame for 5-10 minutes. After cooling the pulp separates from the shell easily, or the pulp can be prized off with a sharp knife. Take care not to cut yourself.

First blend the juice with yogurt (1 ½ cup), cut pieces of pulp, salt (¾ tsp), and sugar (1 tsp) and leave sitting in the electric blender.

In either a small pot or a large ladle, over a medium flame add ghee (1 ladle 45 ml) and make the chaunce (mixture of spices). To the heated ghee add urad dal (2 tsp), fenugreek (1 tsp), curry leaves (10), asafetida (½ tsp), grated ginger (2 tbs) and chopped green chillies (2).

When sizzling pour the chaunce directly into the blender. Add washed fresh coriander leaves (10) to give a very slight green colour to the chutney.

Mix thoroughly so that all the pulp is blended to give a smooth mixture. Remove and serve with a savoury.

Preparation time: 10 min

Ingredients

250 g dates
500 ml water
2 tbs tamarind pulp or
50 g compressed tamarind

1 tsp black salt
1 tsp sugar
½ tsp chilli powder
½ tsp ajwain seeds

Preparation Method

Weigh out dates (250 g) wash and remove the stones. Transfer the dates to a small saucepan and boil in water (500 ml) for 10 minutes over a medium flame. Allow to cool and then transfer from saucepan to an electric blender. Add tamarind pulp (2 tbs) followed by black salt (1 tsp), sugar (1 tsp), chilli powder (½ tsp) and ajwain seeds (½ tsp). Mix thoroughly transfer into small stainless steel bowls and serve with a savoury.

N.B. If tamarind is used from a packet (compressed 50 g), boil with the dates as above in a small saucepan, however this time after flavouring and mixing in a blender filter through a sieve, collect and then transfer into above mentioned bowls and serve.

Preparation time: 10 min

Cooking time: 10 min

Ingredients

2 ½-3 cups yogurt
¾-1 cup cashew nuts
¾ tsp salt
1 tsp sugar
1 tsp lemon juice

2 green chillies
2 tbs grated ginger

Preparation Method

To a liquid blender add yogurt (2 ½-3 cups) followed by cashew nuts (¾-1 cup), not roasted, finely chopped chillies (2), grated ginger (2 tbs), salt (¾ tsp), sugar (1 tsp) and lemon juice (1 tsp).

Mix well in an electric blender until smooth, transfer to small bowls and serve with a savoury.

Preparation time: 5 min

SWEETS

8.1 DAILY SWEETS (MILK POWDER BURFI)

Ingredients

1 kg butter
1 kg sugar

560 ml milk
⅓ cup vanilla essence
1.6-1.7 kg full cream milk powder
2-3 tbs cardamon powder

Preparation Method

N.B. This recipe is for large quantities of sweets (approximately 120) 2 x 2 cm pieces. It can be scaled down accordingly and still maintain the quality.

First grease a stainless steel tray 45 cm x 60 cm with sunflower oil.

Next melt butter (1 kg or 4 x 250 g blocks) in a large karhai / wok over a high flame add sugar (1 kg) to the melted butter and mix with whisk.

The sugar is caramelized, until brownish in colour. This should take approximately 5-10 minutes. Do not over overcook.

Next add ground cardamon (2-3 tbs), [milk (560 ml) along the side of the karhai] and vanilla essence (⅓ cup).

Adjust the heat to a low flame add the full cream milk powder (1 kg) mix and then add the remainder of the milk powder (0.6-0.7 kg). Mix well with a whisk and cook for 10 min.

Transfer the mixture of the karhai / wok to the greased tray by carefully spooning out the contents. Level with a rolling pin to give a smooth finish.

N.B. There have been cases where the fat from the milk can separate from the fat of the butter. To prevent this from happening during the caramelizing of the sugar do not overcook and when the milk is being added, it is best to add the milk along the side of the karhai / wok and not directly over the centre of the bubbling butter and sugar mixture.

Preparation time: 5 min   Cooking time: 20 min

Ingredients

3 cups sugar
1 cup water

2 cups water
1 cup cornflour
pinch of Spanish saffron
few drops yellow food colouring or
¼ tsp of turmeric powder
½ cup melted ghee
3 tbs rose water
¼ cup flaked almonds

Preparation Method

Add water (2 cups) to a mixing jug, followed by cornflour (1 cup) whisk continuously to prevent the formation of a solid lump. Next add a pinch of Spanish saffron and a few drops of yellow food colouring or turmeric (¼ tsp). Continue whisking and allow to stand. Move onto making the sweet syrup.

Melt ghee (½ cup) and set aside.

Dissolve sugar (3 cups) in water (1 cup) over a high flame in a medium sized pot. Stir continuously with a wooden spoon.

Once the sugar has dissolved a thick syrupy mixture will be visible. Lower the flame to medium.

Add the contents of the jug to the thick syrupy sugar mixture stirring continuously, first with a whisk.

During the mixing add the melted ghee (½ cup), rosewater (3 tbs), followed by flaked almonds (¼ cup).

Change to using a square wooden spoon and continue mixing and stirring picking up halva from the sides of the pot and returning it to the centre until a jelly like consistency is obtained.

Transfer the contents of the pot into a medium sized stainless steel tray which has been glazed with oil.

Allow to cool. When fully set cut into 16 pieces, see recipe for ondwa 6.8. Remove the square halva pieces carefully and serve on small plates.

Preparation time: 10 min   Cooking time: 15 min

N.B. Flavourings Spanish saffron and rose water can be replaced by grating an orange and adding the rind to the mixture of water and cornflour.

Ingredients

2.2 litres full fat milk

⅓ cup short or long grain rice

1 cup sugar

Preparation Method

Pour milk (2.2 litres) into a large pot followed by sugar (1 cup). Stir with a square wooden spoon and heat over a medium flame.

Wash short or long grain rice (⅓ cup) in a sieve, under a tap and set aside.

When the sugared milk comes to the boil add all the washed rice immediately and cook for approximately 1 ½-2 hours over a low flame.

Stir and continue stirring at regular intervals every 5-10 minutes scrapping the bottom and sides to prevent sticking and burning.

Cook until the rice begins to bubble in the centre and gives a thick pudding consistency.

After 2 hours of slow cooking the milk should have reduced to two thirds of its original volume.

Remove the pot from the heat and allow cool.

Flavourings:

1. At the beginning of the cooking after the addition of sugar add cinnamon sticks (2-3), bay leaves (2) and cardamons (5) in their shells.

2. Alternatively after sweeting with sugar add 4-5 star shaped aniseeds.

3. After cooking and when cool add vanilla essence (5 ml) mixed with either washed and sliced strawberries (8) or slices of ripe mango pulp (1).

    Do not add cold fruit to hot sweet rice you might see curdling of the milk. It is best to add fruit to sweet rice which has cooled to room temperature.

4. Add Spanish saffron threads (1 tsp) at the beginning of the cooking and after the cooking add cardamon powder (½ tsp).

Ideally sweet rice should be served chilled, the colder the sweet rice the better it tastes. Pour into bowls and serve.

Preparation time: 5 min   Cooking time: 1 ½-2 hr

Ingredients

¾ cup self raising flour
¾ cup icing sugar
¾ cup plain flour

1 tsp cinnamon powder
1 tsp vanilla essence
½-¾ cup cold milk

Yogurt mix
4 cups yogurt
¾ cup caster sugar
1 tsp vanilla essence
250 g strawberries

Preparation Method

To a large mixing bowl add self raising flour (¾ cup), icing sugar (¾ cup), plain flour (¾ cup), cinnamon powder (1 tsp) and vanilla essence (1 tsp).

Next add cold milk (½-¾ cup) slowly to make the batter thick enough to cling to a wooden spoon without dripping off.

Line a colander with kitchen roll to absorb excess ghee.

Fill a karhai / wok or deep-frying pan three quarters with ghee and heat over a medium flame until it is hot but not smoking. There are two ways of adding this batter to the hot ghee.

Scoop out some batter with a tablespoon and push lumps of it into the warm ghee.

Or with 3 fingers take out ball shaped batter and push it into the warm ghee with the thumb.

Using either method put in as many balls into the hot ghee trying to prevent the balls from touching each another.

Deep-fry turning the malpuras over for 6 to 8 minutes until golden brown and crispy, allowing both the inside and the outside of the malpuras to cook evenly.

Remove with a slotted spoon and transfer to the lined colander.

In a mixing bowl beat together yogurt (4 cups), caster sugar (¾ cup), vanilla essence (1 tsp) and sliced fruit (250 g strawberries).

Add the cooked malpuras into the yogurt mix and allow to soak for 1 hour then transfer to bowls and serve.

Preparation time: 10 min   Frying time: 20 min   Soaking time: 60 min

Ingredients

2 cups full fat milk powder
¼ cup semolina
¼ cup self raising flour
160 ml cold milk approx
½ tsp cardamon powder

Syrup
4 cups water
2 cups sugar
½ g or a pinch of Spanish saffron

Preparation Method

Syrup Preparation

Make the sweet syrup first before the dough is prepared.

Bring water (4 cups) to the boil over a medium flame in either a large pot or a large stainless steel mixing bowl. Add sugar (2 cups) and stir to dissolve.

Next add Spanish saffron (a pinch) and continue boiling for a further 10 minutes. When all the sugar has dissolved and the water is yellow in colour turn off the heat and allow to cool.

Dough Preparation

To a large mixing bowl add full fat milk powder (2 cups), semolina (¼ cup), self raising flour (¼ cup) and cardamon powder (½ tsp).

Add cold milk (160 ml) in small amounts and mix to give a flexible dough.

From this dough make approximately 25 mini balls (2.5 cm) in diameter.

Take enough dough for one ball and roll it between the palms of your hands in a circular motion. Do not cup the hands. Use the palms, not the fingers. If some dough sticks to the hand this is a good sign.

While rolling in between your palms for 4 to 5 seconds, gradually release the pressure of the hands while at the same time speeding up the motion. This technique if carried out correctly will give smooth white balls free of cracks. Repeat for the remaining dough.

Set up a karhai / wok or deep-frying pan three quarters full with ghee and heat over a low flame.

Add the rounded milk balls which will sink to the bottom for a minute or two and then rise to the surface again. Keep the small balls from burning on the bottom by turning them over with a slotted spoon.

As the milk balls rise to the surface and float, spin them in the ghee by gently rubbing the top with the back of the slotted spoon to ensure they cook uniformly. Cook for 15-20 minutes.

To test if the gulab jamuns are cooked add one to the syrup if it does not collapse the gulab jumuns are cooked. As a general rule avoid putting cooked gulabs into hot syrup they may all collapse and spoil the preparation.

Fry until brown in colour remove with a slotted spoon and carefully place the balls into the cold syrup. Soak and rotate them in the syrup after 15 minutes so that they will be uniformly sweet, soft and spongy. Total soaking time (30 minutes approximately). To test the gulab jamuas are cooked squeeze one in between your fingers to form a dimple. If the squeezed gulab jamun springs back to its original rounded shape the gulab jamuns are cooked.

Remove with syrup into bowls and serve.

Preparation time: 15 min
Frying time: 15-20 min
Soaking time: 30 min

N.B. Alternative flavourings

1). At the beginning of cooking the syrup add cinnamon stick (1), bay leaves (2) and cardamons (5) in their shells.
2). After cooking during the soaking add rose water (3 tbs).
3). Add one orange rind to the gulam juman dough before rolling and add vanilla essence (1 tbs) to the syrup after cooking and during the soaking.

Spanish Saffron

Ingredients

500 g butter
3 ¾ cup chickpea flour
1 ¼ cup icing sugar
⅓ cup flaked almonds (optional)

Preparation Method

Melt butter (500 g) in a large non-stick pan over a medium flame.

To the melted butter add chickpea flour (3 ¾ cup) cook for 15 minutes stirring continuously using a square wooden spoon. At the beginning of the cooking process you can add a handful of walnuts or hazelnuts.

The golden colour and the smell of cooked chickpea flour indicates that it is cooked.

Instead of adding nuts at the beginning you can add a handful of raisins at the end of the cooking and mix.

Remove from the heat add icing sugar (1 ¼ cup) and mix.

Transfer the cooked chickpea flour to a medium sized stainless steel tray and level out with a spatula. If the ladoo is kept plain sprinkle the top with white poppy seeds or sprinkle with flaked almonds and place the tray on the top shelf of a fridge to harden takes (1- 1 ½ hours approximately).

Remove from the fridge, cut into 16 pieces, place on small plates and serve.

N.B. See recipe for ondwa 6.8 which describes the procedure on how to cut the block into 16 equal pieces.

Preparation time: 5 min   Cooking time: 20 min

8.7 HALVA

Ingredients

1 block butter 250 g
1 ¼ cup coarse semolina
½ cup dark raisins or
8-10 strawberries

3 cups hot water
1 ½ cup white sugar
1 tsp vanilla essence

Preparation Method

Halva is prepared in two pots.

Melt butter (250 g) in a medium sized pot over a medium flame.

Add coarse semolina (1 ¼ cup) and dark raisins (½ cup) or any chopped nuts except peanuts stir and roast to a golden brown colour until the butter begins to separate from the grains.

In another pot over a high flame dissolve sugar (1 ½ cups) in water (3 cups). Slowly pour the hot sugared water into the semolina pot stirring with a wooden spoon.

Be careful the mixture will splutter as the hot water comes in contact with the hot grains.

At this stage chopped fruit (8-10) strawberries can be added if in the beginning no additions were made.

Stir briskly for 2-3 minutes to break up any lumps. Cover and leave to simmer on a low flame for 2-3 minutes until all the liquid has been absorbed into the grains. At the end of the cooking period add vanilla essence (1 tsp) or dry roasted desiccated coconut.

A few quick stirs will help fluff up the halva.

Transfer to bowls and serve hot.

Preparation time: 5 min   Cooking time: 15 min

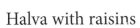
Halva with raisins

8.8 SHRIKHAND (THICK FLAVOURED YOGURT)

Ingredients

8 cups plain yogurt
3-4 tbs milk 50 ml
¼ tsp Spanish saffron
½ tsp ground cardamon
1 ¼ cup caster or icing sugar
2 soft mangos
10 pistachio nuts

Preparation Method

Measure out plain yogurt (8 cups). Pour it into a doubly folded cheese cloth lining a colander and balance it over a bowl to collect the water. Put the bowl with the yogurt in a fridge and allow to drain overnight.

The next morning discard the water collected and work with the thick yogurt remaining in the cheese cloth.

Add Spanish saffron (¼ tsp) to a measuring cup followed by milk (3-4 tbs, 50 ml). Place the cup on a hot plate over and heat over medium flame. Reduce the volume of the milk but not to complete dryness (5 ml approx), remove from the heat. Take care not to burn the milk or the saffron. This procedure helps to melt the saffron giving an aromatic fragrance and a deep yellow colour to the milk.

Transfer the thick yogurt from the colander to a medium sized mixing bowl, add ground cardamon (½ tsp), caster or icing sugar (1 ¼ cup) and finally the saffroned milk. Mix thoroughly. Choose a soft ripe mango, wash, peel and cut into cubes and add it to the sweetened yogurt to enhance the flavor.

Spoon into four medium sized bowls, sprinkle with finally chopped pistachio nuts (10) and serve.

N.B. A similar result can also be obtained with Greek style yogurt which can be purchased from most supermarkets. Follow the recipe from the third paragraphy.

Draining time: overnight   Preparation time: 15 min

8.9 JAGANNATHA TONGUES

Ingredients

1 ½ cups plain flour
½ cup cold water approximately
2 tbs melted ghee
4 tbs chapati flour

½ cup water
1 cup sugar

Preparation Method

This recipe will make approximately 18-20 pieces.

First make the syrup in a medium sized cooking pot.

Chose a small pot and dissolve sugar (1 cup) in water (½ cup) over a medium flame stirring with a wooden spoon. Remove from the heat and allow to cool to room temperature.

Next in a large mixing bowl combine flour (1 ½ cup) with small amounts of cold water (½ cup). It is important to mix with one hand and pour water gradually with the other hand. This will ensure a stiff pastry after kneading.

Divide the dough into two equal halves. Cover one half with the mixing bowl. Sprinkle the work surface with flour.

Roll out the other half of the dough thinly into a square shape approximately 30 x 30 cm and 2-3 mm in thickness.

To the thinly rolled out pastry add lukewarm melted ghee (1 tbs) and spread evenly by hand to cover the entire surface including the edges. Sprinkle with medium chapati flour (2 tbs).

Tightly roll the pastry into a very thin elongated Swiss roll which will lengthen to approximately 45 cm. This is the correct shape for perfect Jagannatha tongues. Cut the ends off and discard.

The rolled up pastry is cut into 2-2 ½ cm segments and kept apart. Each segment is slightly flattened with the palm of the hand and slowly but firmly rolled out into tongue like shapes approximately 6-7 cm long and 3 mm in thickness. It is preferable to roll out all the segments and place them neatly on the table ready for frying.

Fill a karhai / wok or deep-frying pan three quarters with ghee and heat over a low flame similar to the gulab jamun preparations 8.5.

Add as many rolled out pastry tongues into the deep-frying pan and after 5 minutes increase the flame to medium heat. Gently push down on each pastry tongue continuously with a slotted spoon this makes them puff up. Turn them over to avoid burning. The shape will change because they expand and spread in size into elongated stacked layers. Once they are golden brown in colour remove from the heat with a slotted spoon drain off excess ghee and spread them out on a flat tray to cool.

Repeat the above with the other half of the pastry.

Collect all the fried and cooled Jagannatha tongues. Turn each one on its side and carefully spoon in the syrup into the spaces between the stacked layers on one side and repeat by turning them over and fill the other side with the syrup so that all spaces are filled. Carefully place them on plates and serve.

Preparation and frying time: 50 min

Ingredients

8 litres full fat milk for 18-20 pieces
300 ml bottled lemon juice
1 tbs citric acid approx add portionwise

1½ cups sugar
1 gram Spanish saffron
or 2 pinch amounts

Preparation Method

Bring to the boil full fat milk (8 litres) in a large stainless pot over a medium flame. This quantity of milk should make approximately 18-20 pieces of sandesh.

Stir frequently to prevent burning and when the milk comes to the boil, remove the pot away from the flame and add bottled lemon juice (300 ml). White curd / paneer immediately separates out.

If necessary add citric acid (1 tbs) sparingly and stir.

Remove curd / paneer with a slotted spoon and place in a large colander draped with a cheese cloth to separate the paneer from the lemon green coloured whey.

Twist the cheese cloth and place a heavy weight on top, such as a pot full of cold water for 20 minutes to squeeze out residual whey.

Add the pressed paneer to a food processor and blend until smooth in texture.

Eight litres of milk should give 5 ½ cups of smooth paneer.

Next add sugar (1 ¾ cups) and mix for 2-3 minutes to give sweetened paneer. The ideal ratio is 3:1 paneer to sugar.

Keep the mixing to a minimum. Excessive mixing causes the fat to separate from the curd.

Next transfer the sweetened paneer to a large stainless steel frying pan 50 cm in diameter.

Heat over a minimum flame for 5-10 minutes, allowing the sugar to dissolve within the lattice of the paneer by moving frequently and turning using a plastic spatula. You have made sandesh.

If the sandesh appears wet, continue cooking on the lowest flame. Do not increase the flame as the texture will turn grainy similar to the texture of semolina.

In some cases if the sandesh is too wet, turn the heat off and transfer the wet looking sandesh to a large stainless mixing bowl, add either carob powder in small portions and mix with a medium sized plastic spatula or add ground almonds and mix.

Never add milk powder as this would spoil the preparation.

If the sandesh is to dry add condensed milk or double cream and mix.

To flavour with saffron prepare the addition of saffron at the beginning of the cooking process. It is best to use Spanish saffron.

Place a hot plate or tava on a medium flame. Measure out Spanish saffron (1 g) or (two pinch amounts) into a measuring cup and add water (100 ml).

Boil gently for a few minutes until almost all the water has evaporated. From 100 ml to 10 ml.

Saffron is expensive. Take care not to boil dry as this would burn the saffron threads.

Transfer the cooked sandesh to a large stainless mixing bowl add the softened saffron and mix with a plastic spatula or mix the cooked sandesh with the saffron in the food blender (1-2 minutes) to give a deep rich yellow colour.

After the saffron colouring, remove the sandesh from the food processor and place it on the table top and cut off small amounts. Begin to make sandesh balls 5 cm in diameter however no need to remove the sandesh from the large mixing bowl. Small pieces of the yellow coloured sandesh can be cut directly from the bowl to make the balls.

There is a subtle technique in rolling perfectly rounded balls.

Cut a small portion, the size of baseball from the bulk of the yellow coloured sandesh. Begin to shape into a ball by placing the piece of sandesh in between the palms of the right and left hand.

Move the right hand in a clockwise direction and at the same time move the bottom left hand in an anti clockwise direction gently squeezing and releasing the pressure, in this way shape into a perfect ball.

Figure 1

Next choose either one or a selection of wooden stencils see Figure 1. These shaped stencils were purchased in Kolkata, India.

Glaze the surface of the stencil with sunflower oil using a small artist's paint brush.

Position the rounded ball on top of the wooden stencil see Figure 2.

Hold the base of the stencil with fingers of the left hand and rotate anti clockwise, gently tapping with the right hand maintaining a crack free ball like form.

If cracks do appear on the surface of the round ball smooth them out by gently rubbing with fingers or fill the cracks up with condensed milk using a fine artists paintbrush and smooth out with fingers or the rotating hand.

Figure 2

Take a medium sized tray, place the stencil and the rounded ball upside down on the surface of the tray, gently push down and remove the stencil to leave a perfect sandesh.

(Repeat the above procedure with the remaining sandesh to give 20 sandeshs).

N.B. Below is a list of alternative flavours which can be used instead of Spanish saffron:

1. Vanilla essence (1 tsp) and either one lemon or one orange rind.

2. Vanilla essence (1 tsp) and sieved carob powder (2 tbs).

3. Roasted and crushed pistachios (½ cup).

There are two ways of adding these different flavourings.

1. After cooking the sandesh in the large frying pan turn the heat off and add one of the suggested flavourings. Mix and fold with a large plastic spatula. Transfer to a large mixing bowl and shape into balls.

2. Transfer the cooked sandesh to a large mixing bowl. Add one of the suggested flavourings mix and fold with a plastic spatula until ready for shaping into balls.

Preparation and cooking time: 1 ½ -2 hr

Ingredients

6 litres full fat milk for 16 pieces
250 ml bottled lemon juice + 250 ml yogurt
1-2 tsp citric acid approx add in portions
1 ½ tbs cornflour (optional) or
¼ cup of fine semolina (optional)

3 litres water
1 kg sugar
3 tbs rose water

Preparation Method

To a large stainless pot over a medium flame add full fat milk (6 litres) and bring to the boil. Stir frequently to prevent burning. This amount of milk will give 16 pieces of rasagulla.

In a jug make the curdling agent which is a mixture of bottled lemon juice (250 ml) and yogurt (250 ml).

When the milk comes to the boil remove the pot from the flame and add the curdling agent with stirring. White curd / paneer immediately separates out. If needed add citric acid (1-2 tsp) sparingly and stir.

Next prepare the sweetened syrup in either a 35 cm wide bottomed stainless steel bowl or a large pot. Mix water (3 litres) with sugar (1 kg). Bring to the boil with stirring over a high flame then lower to a minimum heat and cover.

Remove the collected curd / paneer with a slotted spoon and place into a 30 cm cone shaped stainless steel colander to separate the curd from the whey.

Wash the curd with cold water and mash the collected paneer with a clenched fist, pressing down with full body weight or use the bottom of a narrow jug. This technique helps to squeeze out the whey and water from the paneer and also helps break up small yellow fatty deposits.

When the paneer is completely whey / water free, transfer the paneer to a food processor and mix for 2 minutes. If the paneer appears to be wet you can add either cornflour (1 ½ tbs) or fine semolina (¼ cup) to give a smooth flexible texture.

Remove the paneer from the food processor and place in a large stainless steel mixing bowl.

Cut off a portion of paneer 3 ½ cm in diameter and begin to shape into a ball by placing a piece of paneer between the palms of the right and left hand.

Like the sandesh preparation 8.10 begin to move the right hand in a clockwise direction and at the same time move the bottom left hand in an anti clockwise direction gently squeezing and shaping into a perfect ball.

Repeat and place at least 16 balls 3 ½ cm in diameter on a stainless steel tray.

Store in a fridge for 5-10 minutes to harden.

Return to the syrup mixture and bring it to the boil again. When the water is boiling add the prepared rasagulla balls to the hot water and cook over a high flame for 15 minutes without a lid.

Rotate the balls gently with a slotted spoon, cover and cook over a minium flame for 30 minutes.

Check every 5 minutes and move gently with a slotted spoon allowing the cooking rasagullas room to expand as the balls increase in size by 30 %.

Half way through the cooking process gently rotate the balls over to ensure even cooking. The rasagullas should be allowed to cook slowly. If needed pour hot water (500 ml) along the side of the pot.

At the end of the cooking process (30-45 minutes) add rose water (3 tbs) to the sweet syrup mixture.

Turn off the heat and leave to stand for at least 2 hours and serve cold.

Preparation and cooking time: 1 hr 15 min

Different brands of rose water

Ingredients

2 cups self raising flour
1 cup coarse semolina powder
1 cup full cream milk powder
50 ml melted ghee
1 cup cold water

3 cups water
2 ¼ cups sugar
2 cinnamon sticks
1 ½ tbs rose water

Preparation Method

Make the fragrant syrup first. To a medium sized saucepan add water (3 cups), cinnamon sticks (2) and sugar (2 ¼ cups). Heat over a medium flame stirring with a wooden spoon until the sugar has dissolved then simmer for 5 minutes. Take the saucepan off the heat and leave to cool. Remove and discard the cinnamon sticks. Stir in rosewater (1 ½ tbs) and leave standing.

Melt ghee (50 ml) in a measuring cup over a medium flame.

Mix self raising flour (2 cups), coarse semolina (1 cup) and full cream milk powder (1 cup) in a large mixing bowl. Make a well in the centre, add ghee (50 ml) followed by cold water (1 cup). Mix by hand and knead to give a dough. Turn the dough out onto a lightly floured surface and continue kneading. Extra ghee or water can be added if needed.

Shape into a French roll 35 cm long and about 8 cm width. Cut into 2.5 cm pieces which should give approximately 16-18 slices.

Line a colander with kitchen roll to absorb excess ghee.

Fill a karhai / wok or a deep-frying pan three quarters with ghee.

Over a medium flame, fry the slices until golden brown. Remove with a slotted spoon to the lined colander.

Place these fried slices in a standard baking tray pour the syrup over allowing the syrup to soak into the slices. Turn them over at regular intervals.

After 30 minutes transfer to bowls with the syrup and serve.

Preparation time: 15 min   Frying time: 20 min

Ingredients

1 cup self raising flour
1 cup plain flour
155 g cold butter
3 tbs caster sugar
¼ cup plain yogurt

1 ½ cup water
1 ½ cup sugar
⅓ cup cornflour
2 tsp lemon rind
½ cup fresh lemon juice
1 drop yellow food colouring or
¼ tsp turmeric
3 tbs butter
350 ml double cream
2 tbs caster sugar
1 tsp vanilla essence

Preparation Method

Step 1
Prepare the pastry first. In large mixing bowl add self raising flour (1 cup), mix with plain flour (1 cup). Next add sliced cold butter (155 g), then caster sugar (3 tbs). Mix all four ingredients by rubbing and mixing between fingers, until a granular texture is obtained. When all the granular texture has passed through the fingers add plain yogurt (¼ cup), mix and knead to give a white dough. Empty the dough out onto the table cover with the mixing bowl and leave to rest.

Step 2
Grate lemon rind from lemons (2). Remove the rinds from grater and set aside. From the same lemons (1 ½) squeeze lemon juice, remove seeds and set aside. Alternatively use bottled lemon juice (½ cup).

Step 3
Return to the pastry roll and shape the pastry into the base of a baking tray large enough for the pastry. Bake in a **preheated oven** at 160°C for 20 minutes. Remove from the oven.

Step 4
To a medium sized pot over a high flame, add water (1 ½ cup), sugar (1 ½ cups) and bring to the boil. Add cornflour (⅓ cup) to this sugary solution stir continuously and bring to the boil again. At the boiling point add the lemon rind, lemon juice and butter (3 tbs). As an option add either yellow food colouring (1 drop) or turmeric (½ tsp). Mix well with a whisk and remove the pot from the heat. Pour the mixture on to the cooled pastry base and spread evenly with a plastic spatula. Place the tray in the fridge for 30 minutes.

Step 5
Whisk double cream (350 ml), caster sugar (2 tbs) and vanilla essence (1 tsp) using a stick blender to give whipped cream. Add the whipped cream to the cooled lemon surface. Spread evenly using a warmed splicing knife to give a smooth finish. Remember to wipe the knife clean in between warming on a hot flame and return to spreading the cream evenly.

Step 6
See the recipe for ondwa 6.8 which describes the method for cutting a cake to get 16 equal pieces. Remove the pieces carefully and serve 4 pieces per plate.

Preparation time: 20 min   Cooking time: 5 min   Baking time: 20 min

Ingredients

1 ½ blocks butter (375 g)
8 cups Scottish porridge oats
2 tsp vanilla essence
½ cup broken or whole hazel nuts
½ cup raisins

1 ¾ cup sugar
1 ½ cup golden syrup

Preparation Method

First melt butter (1 ½ blocks 375 g) in a small pot.

Next in a large mixing bowl add Scottish porridge oats (8 cups), vanilla essence (2 tsp), hazel nuts (½ cup), raisins (½ cup), sugar (1 ¾ cup), golden syrup (1 ½ cups) and the melted butter.

Mix with a large stainless steel spoon.

Grease a large baking tray and cover with a thin layer of semolina to prevent sticking or cover the surface of the baking tray with grease proof paper.

Add the mixture to the baking tray spread and level with a plastic spatula. Bake in a **preheated oven** at 165-170°C for 40 minutes or until golden brown in colour.

To check that the flapjack is cooked insert a small knife into the middle and remove. If the knife is dry the flapjack is cooked. Moisture on the knife indicates the flapjack is not cooked, continue baking for a further 5 minutes.

Allow to cool and refer to ondwa recipe 6.8 which describes how to cut the flapjack into 16 equal pieces.

Remove the pieces carefully and place on serving plates.

Preparation time: 10 min   Baking time: 40 min

8.15 Custard pudding

Ingredients

1.2 litre cold milk
¾ cup white or soft brown sugar

In a mixing jug
250 ml milk
¾ cup cornflour
1 ½ tsp vanilla essence
¼ cup carob powder
1 tbs butter (optional)

Preparation Method

Custard pudding is made in 4 steps:

Step 1
Into a mixing jug add milk (250 ml) followed by cornflour (¾ cup), sieved carob powder (¼ cup), vanilla essence (1 ½ tsp), butter (1 tbs) which is optional, stir and set aside. The butter helps to give the custard a thicker and smoother texture.

Step 2
To a medium sized pot add milk (1.2 litres) followed by white or soft brown sugar (¾ cup) and bring to the boil with stirring over a medium flame.

Step 3
Pour the contents of the jug into the boiling sugared milk.

Whisk to prevent formation of lumps and this mixing also ensures even mixing of vanilla essence.

Switch to a wooden spoon continue mixing and stirring for 5-10 minutes. Turn off the heat and allow to cool to a reasonable temperature for handling purposes.

Step 4
Carefully pour the cooked custard into bowls decorate with slices of strawberries and serve.

N.B. Different flavoured puddings can also be made using either a pinch of Spanish saffron added in step 1 or washed and prepared strawberries (6-12) finely chopped and added after whisking and before using the wooden spoon. Plain custard is made without any flavourings.

Preparation time: 5 min   Cooking time: 20 min

8.16 Sweet custard samosa

Ingredients

1 litre cold milk (4 cups)
¾ cup white sugar
pinch of Spanish saffron

In a mixing jug
1 cup cold milk
¾ cup cornflour
½ cup raisins or
sultanas

Samosa Pastry
3 ½ cups plain flour
½ cup melted ghee
1 cup hot water
3 tbs caster sugar

Preparation Method

Make the custard as described in 8.15 adding raisins or sultans in step 1 and use this as the filling for the samosas.

Prepare the pastry as described in (6.3 fried samosa savory recipe) and fill the empty cone shaped samosa pastry with the prepared custard fold, seal and deep-fry as described in 6.3.

After frying remove and allow to drain and cool in a colander lined with a kitchen roll to absorb excess ghee.

Transfer to four small trays sprinkle with sieved icing sugar and serve.

Preparation time: 30 min   Cooking time: 15 min   Frying time: 20 min

Ingredients

2 cups plain flour
2 cups self raising flour
300 g sliced butter
4 tbs caster sugar
½ cup plain yogurt

18-20 medium sized apples
1 tsp cinnamon powder
¾ cup sugar
¼ cup raisins
1 grated orange rind

Preparation Method

Wash and peel apples (18-20).

Either split the peeled apples into equal slices using an apple splicer or cut into slices.

Transfer the apple slices to a large cooking pan, heat over a medium flame for about 15 minutes to soften.

During the cooking period add cinnamon powder (1 tsp), sugar (¾ cup), raisins (¼ cup) and grated orange rind (1).

Make the pastry in a large mixing bowl with plain flour (2 cups), self raising flour (2 cups), sliced butter (300 g) and caster sugar (4 tbs).

Mix by rubbing and mixing between fingers, until a granular texture is obtained.

Next add plain yogurt (½ cup) and knead by hand to make the sweetened pastry.

Divide this pastry into two halves. One half is rolled out into an oblong shape.

Choose a large baking tray grease the base and sides with oil and sprinkle with semolina.

Insert the oblong shaped pastry into the greased tray and cut to shape the bottom and sides of the tray pushing the pastry well into the corners.

Pierce the entire base with a fork to prevent puffing up and bake in a **preheated oven** at 160°C for 20 minutes.

Remove the cooked base from the oven.

Add the cooked apples (mash if needed) to the pastry base. Spread evenly and then cover with the second rolled pastry positioning into place and sealing all the ends and corners. Remove any excess pastry with a knife.

Brush the top with soured cream, sprinkle with demarara sugar, pierce the top with a fork and bake in an oven at 170°C for 20 minutes.

Remove from the oven, cool and cut into 16 pieces, see ondwa recipe 6.8 which describes how to do this. Carefully place the pieces on trays and serve.

Preparation time: 20 min   Cooling time: 15 min   Baking time: 40 min

8.18 Cheesecake

Ingredients

1 cup self raising flour
1 cup plain flour
150 g sliced cold butter
3 tbs caster sugar
¼ cup plain yogurt

3.5 litres full fat milk
290 ml bottled lemon juice
1 cup soured cream
1 cup caster sugar
2 grated orange rind
2 tsp vanilla essence

500 g strawberries or
8-10 plums
½ cup granulated sugar
1-2 tbs cornflour (optional)

Preparation Method

Step 1
Prepare paneer as described in the recipe for spinach and paneer sabji 3.2. Use full fat milk (3.5 litres) and bottled lemon juice (290 ml). Press the prepared paneer for approximately 5-10 minutes.

Step 2
Make the pastry as described in recipe 8.13 lemon curd tart.

Step 3
Preparation of strawberry jam.

Wash the strawberries (500 g) and remove by hand or cut away the green stalks and slice to give equal pieces, add to a medium sized pot and heat over a medium flame. Next add sugar (½ cup) and cook for 10-15 minutes. There is no need to add water.

If strawberries are not available use plums (8-10) depending on size. Wash the plums cut into half remove the stones cut into segments add to a medium sized pot with sugar (¾ cup) and heat over a medium flame 15 minutes. If water is needed a minimum amount can be added. In some cases the jam might appear to be runny, the texture can be adjusted by adding cornflour (1-2 tbs) and mix.

Step 4
Mix soured cream (1 cup), with the freshly prepared paneer (3 cups), caster sugar (1 cup), grated orange rind (2) and vanilla essence (2 tsp) in a food processor.

Step 5
Return to the pastry, roll it out flat and lay it on the base of the baking tray and trim the edges. Bake the pastry in a **preheated oven** at 160°C for 20 minutes remove from the oven and set aside.

Step 6
When the pastry base has cooled to room temperature add the mixture of step 4 and spread evenly over the base keep in a depth of approximately 3-4 cm, return the tray to the oven and bake for a second time at 160°C for 30-40 minutes. Insert a knife into the middle which should return dry and the top has a light yellow golden colour, allow to cool to room temperature.

Step 7
Spread the cooled strawberry jam gently on top of the cooked cheese. Place in the fridge for 30 minutes. Cut into 16 slices using the method described in ondwa recipe 6.8 and serve on small plates.

Preparation time: 30 min   Baking time: 60 min

8.19 Sponge Cake

Ingredients

3 cups plain flour
1 ½ tsp bicarbonate soda
1 ½ tsp baking powder
3 tbs carob powder (optional)

1 ¼ cups sunflower oil
1 ¼ cups milk
3 tbs yogurt
3 tbs golden syrup
1 ¼ cup sugar
2 tsp vanilla essence
350 ml double cream
8-10 plums or
15 strawberries
½ cup sugar

Preparation Method

First mix the dry ingredients, plain flour (3 cups), bicarbonate soda (1 ½ tsp), baking powder (1 ½ tsp) and carob powder (3 tbs optional) in a medium sized mixing bowl.

In another medium sized bowl / jug add sunflower oil (1 ¼ cups), milk (1 ¼ cups), yogurt (3 tbs), golden syrup (3 tbs), sugar (1 ¼ cups) and vanilla essence (2 tsp) and mix.

Add the wet ingredients to the dry ingredients and mix thoroughly. Transfer the cake mixture to a greased and lightly floured baking tray or line the baking tray with grease-proof paper add a thin coat of sunflower oil and now transfer the cake mixture and spread evenly.

Bake in a **preheated oven** between 170-180°C for 35 minutes.

Check the cake is cooked in the usual way, by pushing a knife into the middle of the cake and remove. If the knife is dry the cake is ready.

If the knife is wet, continue baking for a further 5 minutes. Remove from the oven and cool to room temperature.

While the cake is cooling prepare either strawberry or plum jam as described in jam preparation for a cheese cake recipe 8.18.

Return to the cooled cake cut through the middle horizontally to give two equal halves.

Add the prepared jam to the bottom half of cake spread evenly and cover with the top half of the cake.

Decorate the top with whipped cream (made from whipping double cream 350 ml) and add fresh fruit or dry fruits and nuts to complete the decoration.

Cut into 16 slices, see ondwa recipe 6.8, place four pieces per small plate and serve.

Sixteen cupcakes can be made from the same cake mix. Spoon the cake mixture into the cupcake cases and bake using the same baking conditions as the cake. After baking transfer to a wire tray to cool. Decorate the tops with icing sugar made from mixing icing sugar (1 ½ cups) with orange juice obtained by squeezing half an orange. Add portionwise to give a glue like consistency paste. Cover the tops liberally and serve.

Preparation time: 30 min   Baking time: 35 min

Ingredients

4 cups self raising flour
2 tsp baking powder
220-250 ml milk
100 g butter
1 ½ tsp vanilla essence
5 tbs caster sugar

400 g strawberries or 8 plums
300 ml double cream

Preparation Method

In a mixing bowl add self raising flour (4 cups), sliced butter (100 g) and baking powder (2 tsp). Mix with finger tips to give a granular breadcrumb like texture.

Next add caster sugar (5 tbs) followed by vanilla essence (1 ½ tsp). Knead into a soft dough adding milk slowly approximately (220-250 ml).

Roll the dough out into a large rectangle or circle 1.5 cm thick.

Cut the dough into circles or heart shapes using stainless steel shaped cutters. Roll the trimmings and cut more shapes.

An inverted measuring cup or glass can also be use to cut ring shapes.

Place the shaped pastry on a greased baking tray. Brush the tops with milk and bake in a **preheated oven** at 170-180°C for 15 minutes.

Strawberry or plum jam is prepared as described in recipe 8.18.

Make whipped cream from double cream (300 ml) using a whisk blender.

Remove the scones from the oven and allow to cool. Cut each scone horizontally and fill the bottom half with jam, close with the top half and decorate with whipped cream.

Transfer to small trays and serve.

Preparation time: 15 min   Baking time: 15 min

8.21 Egg Free Meringues

Ingredients

2 ½ cups water
½ cup brown linseed (flaxseed) see page 307
2 tbs fat free skimmed milk powder
1 tbs cornflour
1 ½ cup caster sugar

Custard cream filling
3 cups milk
½ cup cornflour
175 g butter
2 cups icing sugar

This recipe will make 20 double or 40 single meringues.

It is important that all cooking utensils and pots used for this preparation are clean and throughly dry as any grease will spoil the final outcome of the meringues.

Preparation Method

Preheat the oven to 120°C

Add water (2 ½ cups) and linseed (½ cup) to a small pot. Over a medium flame cook for approximately 2 ½ minutes from the point of boiling or until the mixture becomes slimy or jelly like in consistency, approximately 250 ml in volume.

Filter the hot jelly through a sieve into a steel mixing bowl of a food mixer or into a tall bowl to avoid splashing during the whipping process when using a hand mixer. Cool to room temperature. Add fat free skimmed milk powder (2 tbs) and cornflour (1 tbs). Whip for 20-30 minutes starting at a slow speed and then gradually increasing the speed to medium for the food mixer. This speed settings also applies to the hand mixer. It is not advisable to whip by hand.

After 20-30 minutes of continuous whipping the mixture quadruples in size, snow like in colour creating stiff peaks as the mixing forks are lifted. The consistency at this stage will be airy and stiff, sticking to the mixing attachments not dripping off. Now gently fold in caster sugar (1 ½ cups).

Line a baking tray / trays with greaseproof paper. Spoon the white meringue mixture into disposable piping bags and pipe onto the surface of the tray in approximately 3 cm diameter swirl shapes leaving approximately 4 cm between each shape, allowing enough room for expansion during the baking period. Place in the oven and **bake at 120°C** for 2 hours. The meringues are ready when they sound hollow, light and slightly golden at the bottom. Transfer to a cooling tray and serve when cool.

Preparation, cooking and whipping time: 45 min   Baking time: 2 hr

Custard Cream Filling

First bring milk (2 cups) to the boil in a small pan and add from a jug a stirred mix of cornflour (½ cup) and milk (1 cup). Whisk during the addition and bring to the boil. Remove from the heat and set aside to cool to room temperature.

Weigh out butter (175 g) cut into pieces and add to a mixing bowl. Gradually add sieved icing sugar (2 cups) then slowly and gradually, add the prepared custard and mix with a hand mixer to give a soft smooth fluffy texture. It is best not to over mix as this would cause the butter to separate. Transfer to a new piping bag and pipe the cream evenly on the base of one of the meringues and sandwich with the base of another meringue. Repeat with the remaining meringues. Meringues can also be served without fillings.

Preparation time: 20 min

MOTHER KULANGANA'S SWEETS

9.1 GOKULA SWEETS

Ingredients

600 g cocoa butter
2 cups water
300 g sugar

600 g milk powder
80 g carob powder
20 ml vanilla essence

Preparation Method

Choose a large stainless steel baking tray and cover the base with grease proof paper.

Weigh out cocoa butter available as a solid block (600 g) and melt it on a low flame in a stainless steel medium sized pot. A low flame is used as cocoa butter melts very easily.

In another small pot dissolve sugar (300 g) in water (2 cups) over a medium flame.

Weigh out milk powder (600 g) and add it to a food mixer followed by carob powder (80 g). Mix the two powders dry for 5-10 minutes.

Return to the sugared water and make sure the temperature is at 70°C / 155°F. This temperature is critical. At exactly 70°C add the hot water steadily to the mixture of the stirring powders and when all the sugared water has been poured into the food mixer add vanilla essence (20 ml) and continue stirring to give a dark brown slurry. Do not stop the stirring.

Return to the melted cocoa butter and check that the temperature does not exceed 60°C / 140°F. The temperature is critical here again. If the temperature has exceeded 60°C allow to cool down naturally or place the pot of hot melted butter in an open tray or large mixing bowl filled with either cold or iced water.

At exactly 60°C / 140°F pour the melted cocoa butter to the sugared brown slurry at a steady rate, with medium stirring. Continue stirring for a further 10-15 minutes after all the melted butter has been added.

Stop stirring lift the stirrer and carefully remove excess sweet off the paddle into the mixing bowl. Transfer the contents of the bowl using a plastic spatula to the baking tray.

Level the surface with a palette knife and place in a freezer for between 30-60 minutes to cool but not freeze, as a frozen solid block would make cutting very difficult.

Check the texture and when hard enough cut into 16 or more pieces using the procedure described in ondwa recipe 6.8. Transfer to small trays and serve.

Preparation time: 40 min   Cooling and setting time: 30-60 min

9.2 HARD SWEET (BURFI)

Ingredients

4.5 litres / 8 pints goshala milk
1 cup sugar

Preparation Method

In a large stainless steel pot 50 cm, diameter by 30 cm, mix goshala milk (4.5 litres / 8 pints) and sugar (1 cup) and bring to the boil over a medium flame.

Control the overflow by stirring, fanning and skimming the surface with a stainless paddle 90 cm long.

Continue cooking the milk with stirring and scrapping the bottom of the pot until all the water has evaporated leaving a soft fudge. Turn the heat off and continue stirring and scrapping the base. Press the dough with your finger and if the dough does not stick to your finger, the preparation is ready to be removed from the pot.

Carefully lift the pot from the heat and place it on its side on the worktop and remove the fudge like dough with a plastic spatula.

Work the fudge with a stainless steel dough spatula breaking up any lumps, scraping from underneath the fudge and then pressing the collected amount onto the table surface and in this way a smooth texture is obtained.

Transfer the fudge to a standard sized baking tray and spread evenly and level off with a rolling pin.

Allow the fudge to harden, cut into 20 equal sized squares and decorate the top with a suitable stencil, see Fig. 1 recipe 8.10. Remove and serve.

N.B. If the quality of milk is poor you can add double cream (½ cup) to improve the preparation.

Preparation and cooking time: 1 hr 20 min

See The Art Of Indian Vegetarian Cooking by Yamuna Devi page 608-631 for detailed descriptions for all milk sweets.

9.3 Pera

Ingredients

5 litres goshala milk
1 cup of sugar for 3 cups of khoa
½ tbs cardamon powder

www.rajabhoga.com

Preparation Method

In a large stainless steel pot 50 cm diameter x 30 cm, boil goshala milk (5 litres) to frothing over a medium flame stirring continuously with a 90 cm long stainless paddle until the milk reduces to about ¼ of its original volume and most of the water has evaporated.

Continue heating and stirring until the milk thickens to give a dough / fudge like appearance. Lift the pot from the heat and place it on top of a clean work surface remove the dough / fudge using a plastic spatula. Gather the mass together and for every 3 cups of the concentrated mixture add sugar (1 cup) and mix using a spatula. This is **Khoa**. Knead until smooth and transfer it back to the pot add cardamon (½ tbs) and continue gently mixing and heating over a low heat cook until the mixture thickens again and pulls away from the sides of the pot. This is **Pera**.

Lift the pot off the heat and place it on top of a clean work surface and remove the dough / fudge using a plastic spatula.

A soft darker coloured fudge will be obtained similar to the burfi preparation 9.3.

Knead and shape into 20 balls by rolling in between greased palms. See recipe 8.10 which describes how to make perfect sweet balls. Place the balls on a large stainless tray and shape with a wooden stencil see Fig. 1 recipe 8.10 sandesh preparation.

Transfer to plates and serve.

Preparation and cooking time: 1 hr 20 min

Ingredients

17 litres goshala milk will make 40 pieces of sandesh
1.4 litres bottled lemon juice
2 cups yogurt
2 cups sugar

Preparation Method

Boil goshala milk (17 litres) in a large stainless pot, 50 cm diameter x 30 cm in height over a medium flame. Stir the milk with a 90 cm stainless steel paddle.

At the boiling point of the milk add a mixture of yogurt (2 cups) and bottled lemon juice (1.4 litres) in small amounts and the white coloured curd / paneer will separate out.

Transfer the prepared paneer using a slotted spoon to a large colander draped in a cheese cloth.

Twist the cloth with the collected paneer and place a heavy weight (a large pot filled with water) on top of the twisted cheese cloth to squeeze out the whey.

Take 2 large stainless steel mixing bowls. To one of the mixing bowl add the prepared paneer and keep the other bowl empty for now.

Add the freshly prepared paneer in portions to a food processor and blend until the paneer is completely smooth.

Remove all the smooth paneer and set aside in the empty mixing bowl mentioned.

Measure out 3 cups of this smooth paneer and put it back into the food processor. Next add sugar (1 cup) and mix thoroughly making sure all the sugar has mixed with the paneer.

Stop the machine remove the blade carefully and empty the sweetened paneer into one of the empty mixing bowl and cover with a cloth to keep moist.

Repeat this procedure until all the smooth paneer has been mixed with a 3:1 cup ratio of paneer to sugar.

Cook all the sweetened paneer in a heavy based, large frying pan on the lowest possible flame for 10-15 minutes, mixing and turning with a stainless dough spatula until the dough appears to roll from the sides of the frying pan. This is plain sandesh.

At the end of the cooking period remove the pan off the flame transfer the plain sandesh to an empty mixing bowl and cover with a tea towel.

Using a plastic spatula cut off a small portion from the bulk of sandesh 4-5 cm and roll into perfectly shaped balls, see recipe 8.10 for the technique.

Choose either wooden stencils (Fig. 1 recipe 8.10) to shape the sandesh balls or flatten slightly and decorate with edible pastes obtained from Sugarflair which is a UK food colouring manufacturer. Sugarflair colourings are Nut Free, Gluten Free, GMO Free and Fat Free suitable for Vegetarians and Kosher approved by Kedassia.

What has been described above is the preparation of plain sandesh.

Flavoured sandesh is made in two ways by adding either finely grated lemon (1) or finely grated orange rind (1) with vanilla essence (1 tsp) at the beginning of cooking the sweetened paneer **or** by adding powdered vanilla which can be obtained by grinding a stick of vanilla 30 cm long then add this freshly ground powder at the beginning of cooking the sweetened sandesh. See page 307 which shows pods of vanilla.

Mix and turn with a stainless steel dough spatula until the flavoured sandesh rolls off the edges of the pan. This cooking should take between 10-15 minutes.

Take the large frying pan off the heat, transfer the cooked flavoured sandesh to a large mixing bowl cover with a tea towel, cut small portions and make balls as described in 8.10.

Shape the balls with wooden stencils Fig.1 recipe 8.10 or flatten slightly using the smoother side of the wooden stencil and decorate with edible oils.

Alternatively flavour with Spanish saffron. Prepare the saffron as described in 8.10.

Add the softened saffron to the plain sandesh in a large bowl. Mix thoroughly with a plastic spatula to give yellow coloured sandesh.

Make into balls, shape or decorate according to personal tastes with food colouring paste obtained from Sugarflair.

N.B. The sweets are decorated by Sucirani Devi Dasi, Sudevi Sundari Devi Dasi and Vrajavilasini Devi Dasi.

Preparation and cooking time: 2 hr

9.5 Khoa

Ingredients

4.5 litres / 8 pints goshala milk
1 cup sugar

Preparation Method

In a large stainless pot 50 cm diameter by 30 cm in height over a medium flame cook down with stirring goshala milk (4.5 litres / 8 pints) until much of the water (85 %) has evaporated to about one-sixth of its original volume.

Carefully lift the large pot onto the work top tilt the pot on its side and with a plastic spatula remove the solid dough like mass from the pot onto the kitchen worktop.

Add sugar (1 cup), mix and fold with a stainless dough spatula on the work surface until the mixture is soft like cotton. You have made khoa.

When you add khoa to sandesh you are making royal sandesh.

Preparation time: 60 min

Preparation Method

Prepare smooth paneer as described in 9.4 and set aside in a mixing bowl.

Measure out 3 cups of the smooth paneer, add sugar (1 cup) and mix thoroughly in a food processor.

Remove from the processor, place in an empty stainless mixing bowl and set aside.

Repeat this procedure with the remaining smooth paneer, mixing with sugar in the above mentioned quantities ratio 3:1 and set aside in the same mixing bowl.

In heavy based large frying pan begin to cook the prepared sweetened paneer on the lowest possible flame.

Add prepared khoa recipe 9.5 either as a solid lump (¼ cup) or grate a lump of khoa into the cooking sandesh. The ideal ratio mix is sandesh (3 cups) to khoa (¼ cup).

Cook for 10-15 minutes turning and folding with a stainless dough spatula until the dough appears to roll from the sides of the pan.

Flavourings and when to add them are identical to sandesh recipe 9.4 without khoa.

Roll into balls in the palms of your hand as described in 8.10.

Make into balls, shape or decorate according to personal tastes with food colouring paste obtained from Sugarflair.

Preparation and cooking time: 2 hr

SALADS

Ingredients

2 medium sized tomatoes
1 cucumber
½ -1 lettuce
2 medium sized carrots

2 tbs olive oil
2 tsp black salt
¼ tsp black pepper
2 tbs lemon juice
1 tbs Italian herbs

Preparation Method

Wash, peel, and grate carrots (2 medium sized) into a large mixing bowl or alternatively after peeling, cut the carrot into carrot sticks or cubes and add them to the mixing bowl.

Medium sized tomatoes (2) are washed cut into cubes and added to the grated carrots.

Wash and cut into shreds lettuce (1) and add to the tomatoes and shredded carrots.

Wash and peel in strips cucumber (1), cut into cubes and add to the mixing bowl.

Dress the salad with a mixture of olive oil (2 tbs), black salt (2 tsp), black pepper (¼ tsp), lemon juice (2 tbs) and Italian herbs (1 tbs). Mix and serve.

Alternatively dress the salad with whisked soured cream (¾ -1 cup), olive oil (3 tbs), Italian herbs (2 tbs), salt (1 tsp), paprika powder (½ tsp) and ground black pepper (½ tsp). Mix and serve.

N.B. The above is a simple salad which is easily prepared. To make an elaborate salad add cubed avocado or cubed paneer 2 cm square pieces. You can also add roasted sunflower seeds or boiled asparagus. Other additions are boiled / raw baby sweetcorns cut into 3 mm rounds or celery sticks. Green apple (1) cut into segments.

Preparation time: 15 min

Raw baby spinach salad

Raw broccoli salad

Ingredients

2 cucumbers
½ pomegranate or
1 banana or
1 carrot medium sized

2-3 cups yogurt
1 tbs broken mustard seeds (rai)
1 ¼ tsp black salt
½ tsp black pepper
1 tsp sugar
¼ tsp asafetida

Preparation Method

Wash and peel a medium sized cucumber (1) into strips using a potato peeler.

Grate the cucumbers through the large holes of a metal grater into a mixing bowl. Squeeze out all the excess water and transfer the grated cucumber free of water to another mixing bowl.

Add seedlings of a pomegranate (½) to the grated cucumber.

Measure out yogurt (2-3 cups) and add it to the grated cucumber followed by yellow broken mustard seeds known as rai (1 tbs), black salt (1 ¼ tsp), black pepper (½ tsp) and asafetida (¼ tsp). To sweeten slightly add sugar (1 tsp), mix thoroughly and serve.

If a pomegrante is not available use a banana.

Wash and peel one banana cut lengthwise, into four quarters and cut again into 5 mm slices.

Add the sliced banana or washed peeled and grated carrot (1) medium sized to the grated cucumber.

Mix in the mentioned ingredients above and serve.

If yellow broken mustard seeds (rai) are not available, place a small ladle over a medium flame add ghee (10 ml). Next add the mustard seeds (½ tsp), let the seeds pop, mix with asafetida (¼ tsp), transfer hot to the yogurt mix with the other ingredients described and serve.

Preparation time: 15 min

FRUIT SALADS

(A limited selection of fruit perparations)

Preparation Method

Choose pineapples (1-2) depending on size.

Wash, top and tail the pineapple 2 cm from the top and bottom and sit it flat on one of the surface. Next shave the sides off by removing the outer skin carefully cutting along the sides of the pineapple. Use the tip of a potato peeler to remove residual bits of skin still found on the body of the pineapple.

Cut the pineapple in half and each half is cut again further into two equal halves to give four quarters. Turn each quarter on its side and cut and discard the hard spine.

The 4 quarters are cut again into 2 equal halves, giving a total of 8 segments.

Cut these segments into 3 cm pieces to fill 4 medium sized bowls and serve.

Preparation time: 15 min

Preparation Method

Melons come in different varieties such as Cantaloupe, Charantais, Galia, Honeydew and Musk Melon.

Depending on what is available choose a melon (1-2) size dependent, wash, top and tail similar to cutting a pineapple. Place the melon in an upright position and shave the sides off by cutting along the sides remove the skin and discard.

Cut the skinned melon into half and then quarters remove the seeds with a spoon. The 4 quarters are cut again into 2 equal halves giving a total of 8 segments and each segment is then cut into 3 cm pieces.

Fill medium sized bowls and serve.

Preparation time: 10 min

Preparation Method

½ -1 watermelon

Take a watermelon (½ -1) depending on the size. Wash and cut into 4 quarters and each quarter is cut into equal slices similar to cutting a loaf of bread. Spread the slices of melon with seeds on 4 small serving trays and serve.

Alternatively the melon can be cut similar to cutting a pineapple or a melon.

Wash top and tail and follow the steps as described in 11.1 and 11.2.

Preparation time: 10 min

Preparation Method

1 kg seedless grapes

Wash grapes (1 kg) remove the stems, put into bowls and serve. Larger grapes are best cut in half. Grapes with seeds are best served with the seeds removed.

Preparation time: 10 min

BEVERAGES

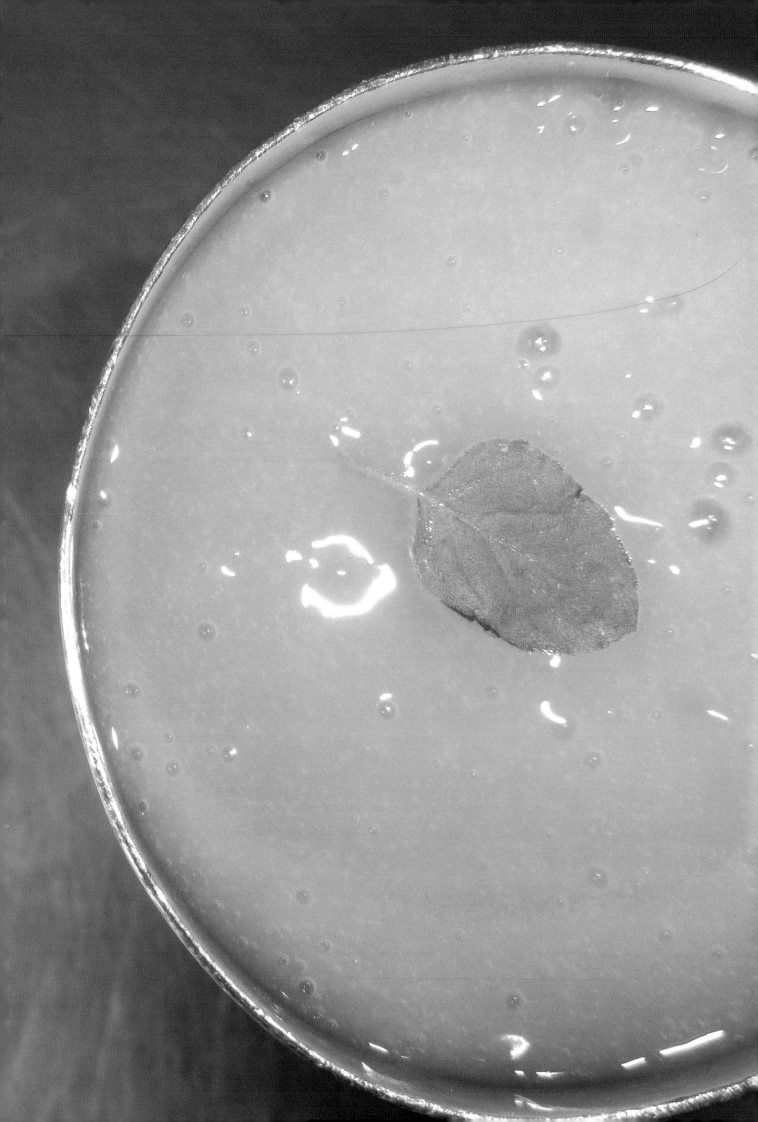

Preparation Method

Fifteen to twenty apples will give approximately 1.2 litres of apple juice.

Wash remove labels and cut into equal halves or use whole depending on the size. Try to remove the stalks however, it is not necessary to remove the skin or the seeds.

Set up the juice maker placing a receiver carefully below the spout and add the whole or cut apples to the spinning electric juicer. Push down on the plunger and collect the juice.

When approximately 1.2 litres has been extracted from the apples add ginger (2-3 tbs) and pass it through the juicer to give ginger flavoured apple juice.

Pour the juice into a jug and chill in the fridge for an hour. Remove froth and discard, or decant carefully into another jug. Pour the juice into cups and serve.

Other options are a mixture of apple and carrot juice using 8-10 apples and 8-10 medium sized carrot sticks with ginger (2 tbs) or straight carrot juice from washed sticks of carrot (15-20) and mixed with crushed fresh ginger (2 tbs) all passed through a juicing machine or apple (8-10) and pears (8-10) passed through the juicer.

Preparation time: 20 min

Preparation Method

15-20 oranges approx
¼ cup sugar (optional)

Take oranges (15-20), wash and cut horizontally into two halves. With the aid of an electric orange juice machine squeeze the juice from the oranges and collect. Transfer, discarding the seeds to a jug. When 1.2 litres has been collected, sweeten with sugar (¼ cup), mix thoroughly and store in the fridge ready to be served. A manual juicer can also be used which will take longer to do. Orange juice can also be served without adding sugar.

Preparation time: 20 min

Preparation Method

2 lemons
1 litre filtered water
½ cup white sugar
fresh mint leaves (optional)

Take lemons (2), wash and cut into 2 equal halves. Squeeze out the juice using either a hand juicer or an electric juice maker. Transfer the collected juice to an electric blender, add filtered water (1 litre), sugar (½ cup) and mix thoroughly.

Add fresh mint leaves (this is optional). Cool in the fridge and serve later.

Preparation time: 10 min

Ingredients

½ litre yogurt
½ litre filtered water
6-8 strawberries
1 tsp vanilla essence
⅓ cup sugar

Preparation Method

Wash and remove the stalks from strawberries (6-8) and add to an electric blender followed by yogurt (½ litre), filtered water (½ litre), vanilla essence (1 tsp) and white sugar (⅓ cup).

Mix thoroughly pass through a sieve and pour the filtered lassi into cups and serve.

Preparation time: 10 min

Ingredients

2 bananas
1 litre full fat pasteurized milk
1 tsp vanilla essence
¼ cup sugar

Preparation Method

Take 2 bananas, wash and peel, cut in half and place in an electric blender. Add full fat pasteurized milk (1 litre), vanilla essence (5 ml) and sugar (¼ cup). Mix thoroughly and pour into cups and serve.

N.B. The following fruits can also be used for this milkshake preparation. Avocado pair (1) or strawberries (50 g) or blackberries (50 g) or blueberries (50 g).

Preparation time: 10 min

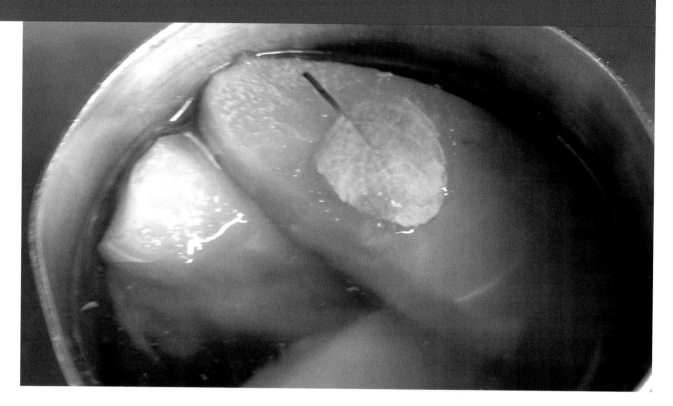

Ingredients

2 litres water
1 large cinnamon stick

3 apples
⅓ cup white sugar or 2-3 tbs honey

Preparation Method

Wash and cut apples (3) into equal sized slices. Remove the seeds and discard. Add the sliced apples to a large pot filled with water (2 litres).

Next add 1 large cinnamon stick, followed by sugar (⅓ cup) and boil for 20-25 minutes. Remove the cinnamon stick pour the entire mixture into an electric blender. After mixing transfer to a jug pour into cups and serve similar to a smoothie or filter through a sieve and serve.

Alternatively do not blend, pass through a sieve and collect the hot apple punch. Pour into cups and serve.

Another option is to serve the juice with the apples.

Preparation time: 5 min

Boiling time: 20-25 min

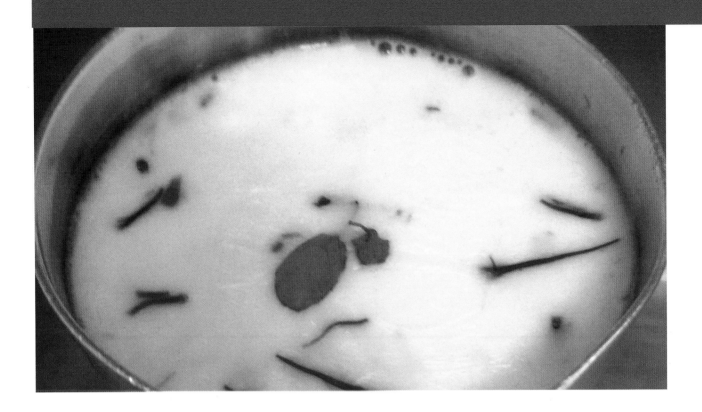

Ingredients

1.2 litres full fat milk
a few strands of Spanish saffron or
1 cinnamon stick
⅓ cup white sugar or 2-3 tbs honey

Preparation Method

Pour full fat milk (1.2 litres) into a medium sized pot.

Add either a few strands of saffron or 1 large cinnamon stick and bring to the boil over a medium flame.

Next add white sugar (⅓ cup) or honey (2-3 tbs).

Bring to the boil again and continue stirring to dissolve the sugar. Remove the cinnamon stick before serving. Best to serve hot.

Preparation time: 5 min   Boiling time: 10 min

EKADASI PREPARATIONS

(A limited selection of Ekadasi recipes)

13.1 EKADASI CHAPATI

Ingredients

3 cups buckwheat flour   or   4 cups farali flour
1 cup potato starch (farina)   ½ cup yogurt
½ cup yogurt   1 tbs sunflower oil
1 tbs sunflower oil   1 tsp salt
1 tsp salt   1 cup hot water (approx)
1 cup hot water (approx)

Preparation Method

Add buckwheat flour (3 cups) and potato starch (1 cup) to a mixing bowl followed by plain yogurt (½ cup), sunflower oil (1 tbs), salt (1 tsp) and hot water (1 cup approximately).

Mix together by hand adding small amounts of hot water to give a smooth dough.

An alternative option is to use farali flour. Begin by adding farali flour (4 cups) to a large mixing bowl followed by yogurt (½ cup), sunflower oil (1 tbs), salt (1 tsp), hot water (1 cup) and mix to give a smooth dough. Divide into 16 equal pieces see chapati preparation 5.1

You need to take extra care with rolling as these doughs are a lot softer than ordinary chapati dough and it can stick to the surface.

The method for cooking is identical to that described in chapati preparation 5.1. Take extra care when cooking as these chapatis can tear easily.

Remove from heat, butter the surface and serve.

Preparation time: 20 min   Cooking time: 20 min

N.B. Farali flour is a mixture of rajigro, samo and sindora (chestnut) flours. Available from Indian shops.

Ingredients

1 cup buckwheat
2 ½ cups hot water
½ cup cashew or peanuts
1 green pepper
1 finely chopped carrot

45 ml ghee
1 chopped green chilli

Preparation Method

Take green pepper (1) wash and cut into two pieces, remove the seeds and cut into 1 cm pieces.

Wash the carrot peel and cut into 1 cm pieces and then set aside.

Fancy whole buckwheat kasha is prepared in the same way as fancy rice see 1.2.

Bring water to the boil (2 ½ cups) in a small pot over a medium flame and while the water is coming to the boil add ghee (1 ladle 45 ml) to a second medium sized pot over a high flame.

To the warming ghee add finely chopped green pepper, carrot and cashew nuts or peanuts (½ cup). Stir for about 2-3 minutes add the washed buckwheat kasha and stir for 1-2 minutes to coat it with ghee.

Add the heated water, cover with a lid and allow to cook over a low flame undisturbed for 20 minutes.

Transfer to bowls and serve.

Preparation time: 5 min   Cooking time: 20 min

Buckwheat

Ingredients

2.2 litres full fat milk

⅓ cup samo seeds

1 cup sugar

pinch of Spanish saffron

½ tsp cardamon powder

⅓ cup flaked almonds

Preparation Method

Pour milk (2.2 litres) into a large pot followed by sugar (1 cup). Stir with a square wooden spoon and heat over a medium flame.

Meanwhile take samo seeds (⅓ cup), wash under a tap in a sieve and set aside.

When the sugared milk comes to the boil add the washed samo seeds and cook for approximately 40-60 minutes, stirring with a wooden spoon and continue stirring at 5-10 minutes intervals, scrapping the bottom and sides to prevent sticking and burning.

Cook until samo seeds begins to bubble in the middle and gives a thick pudding consistency.

The milk should have reduced to ⅔ its original volume. Remove the pot from the heat and allow to cool.

Flavourings:

1. Add a pinch of Spanish saffron at the beginning of the cooking. At the end of the cooking sprinkle with cardamon powder (½ tsp), flaked almonds (⅓ cup), mix and serve.

2. Add cinnamon sticks (2-3), 2 bay leaves and cardamons (5) in their shells at the beginning.

Pour into bowls and serve.

Preparation time: 5 min   Cooking time: 40-60 min

Ingredients

1.5 litres full fat milk
125 ml bottled lemon juice
16 tomatoes
1 medium sized courgette or
1 green pepper

2 tbs olive oil
1 chopped green chilli
2 tbs grated ginger
1 tsp black pepper
1 tsp salt
½ tsp paprika powder
1 tbs Italian herbs

Preparation Method

First prepare paneer as described in recipe 3.2 using full fat milk (1.5 litres) and bottled lemon juice (125 ml).

Press the prepared paneer for approximately 10 minutes.

Transfer paneer from the cheese cloth into a large mixing bowl and set aside.

Choose 16 medium sized tomatoes. Slice off the top third of the tomatoes and keep this will serve as the 'lid' for the stuffed tomatoes.

Cut around the edge of the tomatoes and scoop out the pulp and set aside in an electric blender for chutney.

At this stage you should have 16 empty tomato shells sitting on cup-cake trays.

Preheat the oven to 150°C.

Next cut into small pieces less than 1 cm in length either a medium sized courgette (1) or a medium sized green pepper (1).

In a small pot, over a medium flame add olive oil (2 tbs), followed by finely chopped medium sized courgette (1) or the finely chopped green pepper (1).

Next add chopped green chilli (1) and freshly grated ginger (2 tbs).

Cook for 3 minutes to soften the vegetable. After this short cooking time pour the contents of the small pot on top of the freshly prepared paneer. Add salt (1 tsp), black pepper (1 tsp), paprika powder (½ tsp), Italian herbs (1 tbs) and mix thoroughly.

Take care, the marinated vegetables with the paneer will be hot. Transfer this filling to a flat medium sized baking tray and spread evenly using a plastic spatula and divide into 16 equal portions, see recipe 6.3.

With a table spoon fill the empty tomato shells. Replace the tops of the tomatoes and bake in a preheated oven for 10-15 minutes at 150°C.

Once cooked allow to cool transfer to small plates and serve.

Preparation time: 20 min   Baking time: 10-15 min

13.5 TOMATO SOUP AND MOGO / CASSAVA CHIPS

Ingredients

10 large or 14 small tomatoes
2 small potatoes
1 large or 2 small carrots
¾ cup single cream
1 litre full fat milk for paneer
85 ml bottled lemon juice
1 red pepper (optional)
1 celery stick (optional)

45 ml ghee or olive oil
1 tsp cumin seeds
1 tsp black pepper
1 tbs grated ginger
¼ tsp cinnamon powder
1 litre water

Preparation Method

Blanch tomatoes (10 large or 14 small) or boil them with the skins on and use without removing the skin.

Take small potatoes (2) wash remove the skin and cut into cubes. Wash and peel a carrot (1 large or 2 small) and cut into cubes. Optional extras which can be used are washed and cubed red pepper (1) and celery stick (1).

First add ghee or olive oil (45 ml) to a medium sized saucepan followed by cumin seeds (1 tsp) and allow to sizzle. Next add black pepper (1 tsp), grated ginger (1 tbs) and stir over a medium flame. Add all the prepared vegetables to the ghee mixture and roast for 5-10 minutes.

Next add the softened tomatoes followed by salt (1 tsp), cinnamon powder (¼ tsp) and water (1 litre) cover and bring to the boil. Continue boiling until all the vegetables are soft. Blend with a stick blender, add single cream (¾ cup) stir.

Cubes of freshly prepared paneer made from full fat milk (1 litre) and bottled lemon juice (85 ml), see recipe 3.2 can also be added to this soup at the end stir and serve.

Preparation time: 10 min   Cooking time: 20 min

The tomato soup can be complimented with **mogo / cassava chips**.

Take cassava root (2 large or 3 medium) wash and cut into half to fit a large pot. Immerse in water boil for almost one hour over a high flame. The outer skin of the root will begin to separate from the flesh. Take care not to overcook.
Remove from the heat carefully, drain the hot water and allow to cool.

Line a colander with kitchen roll to absorb excess ghee.

When the cooked root cassava has cooled down, peel off the skin carefully then top and tail. Cut into half lengthwise. Remove the core string and cut into small chips 5-6 cm lengths.

Deep fry in a karhai / wok or deep-frying pan three quarters full with ghee over a high flame until golden. Remove with a slotted spoon drain and transfer to a lined colander. Add black salt (2 tsp), black pepper (1 tsp), paprika powder (½ tsp), chilli powder (½ tsp), sprinkle with lemon juice (2 tbs), toss and serve.

Boiling time: 60 min   Frying time: 15 min

Ingredients

1.2 litre cold milk
¾ cup white or soft brown sugar
pinch of Spanish saffron (optional)

In a mixing jug
¾ cup potato starch also called farina
250 ml milk
1 tsp cardamon powder

Preparation Method

Custard Pudding is made in 4 steps

Step 1
To a medium sized pot add cold milk (1.2 litres) then add white or soft brown sugar (¾ cup). Sir and bring to the boil over a medium flame. A pinch of Spanish saffron can be added - this is optional.

Step 2
Pour milk (250 ml) into a mixing jug followed by potato starch also called farina (½ cup) and cardamon powder (1 tsp). Mix thoroughly and set aside.

Step 3
Pour the contents of the jug into the boiling sugared milk, whisking vigorously to stop lumps from forming and ensuring uniform spreading of the cardamon powder.

Cook for a further 5-10 minutes change the whisk for with a square wooden spoon and continue stirring and scrapping along the sides and the bottom.

Turn off the heat and allow to cool to a reasonable temperature for handling purposes.

Step 4
Carefully pour the cooked custard into bowls, cool to room temperature and serve.

Additional options are a pinch of saffron or washed and chopped pieces of strawberries (2) see recipe 8.15 custard pudding.

Preparation time: 5 min   Cooking time: 20 min

13.7 Coconut cake

Ingredients

2 ½ cups fine coconut
2 cups potato starch also called farina
3 cups milk powder
2 ½ cups cold milk
2 tsp bicarbonate soda
4 tbs soured cream or plain yogurt
1 ½ cups sugar
1 tsp almond essence (optional)
handful green raisins (optional)
125 g melted butter

700 g strawberries or
500 g plums
300 ml double cream
2 tbs caster sugar

Preparation Method

Preheat the oven to 160°C.

Melt butter (125 g) in a small pot over a medium first.

To a large mixing bowl add fine coconut powder (2 ½ cups) followed by potato starch also called farina (2 cups), milk powder (3 cups), cold milk (2 ½ cups), bicarbonate soda (2 tsp), soured cream or plain yogurt (4 tbs), sugar (1 ½ cup), almond essence (1 tsp) and a handful of green raisins.

Mix with a plastic spatula or wooden spoon and after mixing transfer the cake mixture to large greased baking tray and spread evenly. Bake in an oven for 30 minutes at 160°C.

To check the cake is ready insert a knife into the centre of the cake, if the knife edge is dry the cake is ready. If moist return to the oven for a further 5 minutes.

After baking remove the cake from the oven allow to cool and cut along the edges of the baking tray. Tip the cake out onto a cooling tray and then turn it back to its original position and allow to cool.

Jam preparation:

Wash and remove the green stalks and leaves from strawberries (700 g), cut into segments and add to a medium sized pot. If strawberries are not available take plums (500 g) remove the stones and cut into equal segments.

Heat either the strawberries or the plum segments for 5 minutes over a medium flame with sugar (½ cup) until soft. Blend with a stick blender and allow to cool.

Slice the cooled cake through the middle and evenly spread the strawberry or plum jam on the bottom half of the cake and then replace the top half.

Decorate the top with a mixture of whipped double cream (300 ml) and caster sugar (2 tbs). Further decorate with sliced strawberries or grape segments.

Cut the cake, refer to recipe for ondwa savoury 6.8 which describes how to obtain 16 equal pieces. Place the pieces carefully on trays and serve.

Preparation time: 10 min   Baking time: 30 min   Decorating time: 15 min

13.8 CASHEW NUT BURFI

Ingredients

5 ½ cups cashew nuts
1 ⅓ cups sugar
1 ¼ cups milk
2 tbs rose water
6-8 broken pistachio nuts

Preparation Method

In a food processor blend cashew nuts (5 ½ cups) to a fine powder. The finer the powder the better the burfi. Leave to stand in the processor and continue with the recipe.

In a medium sized pot mix milk (1 ¼ cups) with sugar (1 ⅓ cups) and cook for 5-10 minutes over a medium flame until a sample taken between the thumb and the first index finger creates a sticky glue like feeling across the fingers. The sticky feeling is important for the burfi preparation. Take care the mixture is hot.

Next add rose water (2 tbs), followed by the finely ground cashew nuts (5 cups), leaving about (½ cup) behind which will be used if the mixture appears wet. Mix these ingredients with a wooden spoon.

Glaze a clean stainless steel work top with sunflower oil. Use a large plastic spatula to remove the mixture from the pot onto the work top.

Glaze a large plastic rolling pin with sunflower oil and begin to roll out the mound of sweetened cashew nuts as thinly as possible (2-3 mm) thick into either an oblong or circular shape 50 x 50 cm.

Take 6-8 pistachio nuts cut into small pieces, sprinkle and roll into the surface evenly.

Allow the burfi to cool and set which could take up to a maximum of 2 hours.

When cold cut into diamond shapes see recipe for kathmir vada 6.6 which describes how to get these diamond shapes.

Use a stainless steel spatula gently push under the sticky burfi maintaining the diamond shape. Place on small plates and serve.

Preparation and cooling time: 2 hr   Cooking time: 10 min

Ingredients

12 carrots approximately
½ block butter (125 g)
10 dates without the stones
½ litre milk
1 ½ cups sugar
1-2 orange rind

Preparation Method

Wash and peel medium sized carrots (12) using a potato peeler.

Grate the carrots in a mixing bowl using the larger holes of the grater or cut the peeled carrots into segments and blend in a food processor. Of the two methods grated carrots is better but takes slightly longer to prepare.

In a flat shaped large saucepan over a medium flame, melt butter (125 g) and when the butter has melted add the blended or grated carrots and mix with a wooden spoon. Flavour the cooking carrots with the rind of two oranges, using the smaller holes of the grater.

In a second pot over a medium flame dissolve white sugar (1 ½ cups) in boiling milk (½ litre). Stirring at regular intervals.

After 5-10 minutes the carrots look golden in colour and cooking in its own juice. Now add the sugared hot milk slowly and cook for a further 20 minutes with stirring.

Take dates (10), remove the stones and cut into 4 quarters. Add them to the cooked carrot which is now orange / red in colour. Mix transfer to bowls and serve.

N.B. It is important not to add the cut dates at the beginning of the cooking period as this would spoil the colour of the carrot halva.

Preparation time: 15 min   Cooking time: 20 min

GLOSSARY

Acharya: a spiritual master who teaches by example.

Ajwain seeds: also known as *ajown* or bishops weed. The plant has a similarity to parsley. A celery-sized spice seed (*Carum ajown*) closely related to caraway and cumin. Raw ajwain smells almost like thyme, but is more aromatic and less subtle in taste as well as slightly bitter and pungent. Ajwain aids digestion and is used to relieve stomach problems. Available from health food stores and all Oriental groceries.

Aniseed-Anise seeds: is considered a spice with a sweet liquorice-like taste. It is of the Family *Apiaceae*, which makes it a relative of other plants like celery, dill, coriander and cumin. Both seed and leaves from the plant *pimpinella anisum* carry the liquorice taste, but in recipes, either whole or ground seeds are usually used to add distinctive flavors to food, drinks and sweets.

Arati: provides an opportunity for all devotees to serve the Deity by playing hand cymbals drums and other musical intruments while singing devotional songs and dancing to glorify the Lord. Meanwhilea pujari offers various articles in graceful circles to the Deities.

Asafetida: also known as *hing* a strong-smelling spice used in small quantities to flavour savouries and vegetables dishes. Asafetida is extracted from the stems of giant perennial plants that grow wild in Central Asia. The resin like gum comes from the dried sap. The resin is greyish-white when fresh but dries to a dark amber colour. The most commonly available form is compounded asafetida, a fine powder containing 30% asafetida resin, along with rice flour and gum Arabic.

Basmati rice: the word basmati in Sanskrit means "the fragrant one" but it can also mean "the soft rice". India is the largest cultivator, consumer and exporter of this rice; it is primarily grown through paddy field farming in the Punjab region. The grains of basmati rice are longer than most other types of rice. Cooked grains of basmati rice are characteristically free flowing rather than sticky, as with most long grain rice. Cooked basmati rice can be uniquely identified by its fragrance.

Bay leaf: or the plural (bay leaves), the leaves of an aromatic tree or bush (*Laurus nobilis*). Fresh or dried leaves are used in cooking for their distinctive flavour and fragrance. The fresh leaves are very mild and do not develop their full flavour until several weeks after picking and drying.

Bhakti: in Hinduism and Buddhism is religious devotion in the form of active involvement of a devotee in worship of the divine.

Bhaktivedanta Manor: is the UK headquarters of the International Society for Krishna Consciousness (ISKCON). The society propagates the teachings of the authentic Vedic scriptures. These were finally brought to the West by Srila Prabhupada the Society's founder. George Harrison of "The Beatles" kindly donated the Bhaktivedanta Manor to ISKCON in 1973 to cater for the growing congregation.

Black salt or *Kala Namak*: it is not actually black but reddish grey in colour due to the presence of trace minerals and iron. It is not used to replace sea or table salt because it has a distinctive flavour. Black salt is used extensively in South Asia cuisines in raitas, chutneys and salads. Available from Indian stores.

Black pepper: comes from a climbing vine, the fruits of which small round berries ripen from green to red and finally to brown. Black peppercorns are actually berries that are picked when they're just turning red. They are then dried whole before being sold. Peppercorns can be green, white or black, depending on when they are harvested.

Brahmacari: a celibate monk the first of the four *asharams* or spiritual orders of life.

Brahmana: an intelligent man who understands the spiritual purpose of life and can instruct others; the first Vedic social order or *varna*.

Buckwheat: known as *kutu* or *phaphra*, it is the triangular shaped seed from any plant of *Genus fagopyrom*. Native to Russia, Ukaraine, Poland, China and Nepal. On Hindu fasting days northern states of India eat items made of buckwheat flour, because, unlike wheat or rice, buckwheat is not a cereal and thus deemed acceptable. Cereals are not generally eaten during Hindu fast days. The buckwheat plants grow quickly and it is rich in iron and contains a large range of B-complex vitamins. Available from Polish and Indian stores. Buckwheat is also sometimes referred to as *kasha*.

Burfi: an Indian sweet.

Cardamon: refers to several plants of the genera *Elettaria* and *Amomum* in the ginger family Zingiberaceae. Both genera are native to India and Bhutan; they are recognised by their small seed pod, triangular in cross-section and spindle-shaped, with a thin papery outer shell and small black seeds. Today, the majority of cardamon is still grown in southern India, although some other countries, such as Guatemala and Sri Lanka, have also begun to cultivate it. Cardamon is the world's third most costly spice topped only by saffron and vanilla. Mostly used to flavour sweets, cardamon has a strong unique taste with an intensely aromatic flavour.

Carob: *Ceratonia siliqua*, the scientific name of the carob tree, derives from the Greek kerátion "fruit of the carob" (from *keras* "horn"), and Latin *siliqua* "pod carob." The term "carat", the unit by which gem weight is measured, is also derived from the Greek word kerátion alluding to an ancient practice of weighing gold and gemstones against the seeds of the carob tree by people in the Middle East. The system was eventually standardized and one carat was fixed at 0.2 grams. Carob is the edible beans of the carob tree in the pea family. The tree is native to the Mediterranean region. Carob powder is rich in protein and also contains pectin and is used as a substitute for cocoa powder.

Cassava: also known as mogo is a long tapered root with a firm homogeneous flesh encased in a detachable rind, about 1 mm thick, rough and brown on the outside. Commercial varieties can be 5 to 10 cm in diameter at the top and around 15 cm to 30 cm long. A woody cordon runs along the root's axis. The flesh can be chalk-white or yellowish. Cassava roots are very rich in starch and contain significant amounts of calcium (50 mg / 100 g), phosphorus (40 mg / 100 g), vitamin C (25 mg / 100 g). However they are poor in protein and other nutrients.

Chana: is a dal and is produced by removing the outer layer of *kala chana* (black chickpeas) and then splitting the kernel. Although machines can do this, it can also be done at home by soaking the whole chickpeas and removing the loose skins by rubbing.

Chapati: is a flat round whole-wheat bread cooked on a hot plate and held over a hot plate until it inflates like a balloon.

Chaunce: also means masala, a mixture of cooked spices.

Chillis: nearly all of our recipes use finely chopped green chillies. It is the fruit of plants from the genus *Capsicum*, members of the nightshade family, *Solanaceae*. The term in British English and in Australia, New Zealand, India, Malaysia and other Asian countries is just chilli without pepper. Chilli peppers have been a part of the human diet in the Americas since at least 7500 BC. Chillies are a mainstay ingredient in a Vedic kitchen valued for its colour flavour and heat. They are rich in Vitamin A and C, renowned for stimulating the digestive process.

Chickpea flour: known as gram flour or besan are often sold under these names in Indian grocery stores and some supermarkets. It is finely milled, almost pale yellow in colour, made from roasted channa dal (*Cicer arietinum*) and is widely used as a binding agent in batters for vegetable fritters known as pakoras and also used in making savouries.

Cinnamon: is a spice obtained from the inner bark of several trees from the genus *Cinnamomum* that is used in both sweet and savoury foods. Cinnamon trees are native to South East Asia. When the bark of the tree is ground to a powder it becomes an important part of a North Indian spice blend called garam masala. Cinnamon quills or better known as sticks are made from stripped-off bark which is flattened and planed away then dried.

Citric acid: is a commodity chemical. More than a million tonnes are produced every year by fermentation. It is used mainly as an acidifier, as a flavouring and as a chelating agent. We use citric acid in small quantities to curdle milk to make home made paneer. Citric acid is a white crystalline sugar like solid and is found naturally in citrus fruits like lemon, limes and oranges.

Cloves: known as *laung* are the nail-shaped dried buds from the sea-loving evergreen tree. Cloves can be used in cooking either whole or in a ground form, but as they are extremely strong, and should be used sparingly. Cloves are also a prominent ingredient in garam masala and have many medicinal uses.

Cocoa butter: also called theobroma oil, is a pale-yellow, pure edible vegetable fat extracted from the cocoa bean. It is used to make chocolate, biscuits and baked goods, as well as some pharmaceuticals, ointments and toiletries. Cocoa butter has a mild chocolate flavour and aroma. Cocoa butter is obtained from either whole cacao beans, which are fermented, roasted and then separated from their hulls. About 54–58% of the residue is cocoa butter. Chocolate liquor is pressed to separate the cocoa butter from the cocoa solids. The Broma process is used to extract cocoa butter from ground cacao beans. Cocoa butter is usually deodorized to remove its strong and undesirable taste. Cocoa butter is the major ingredient in the commercial production of both white chocolate and milk chocolate. The most common form of cocoa butter has a melting point of around 34-38 °C (93-100°F), rendering chocolate a solid at room temperature that readily melts once inside the mouth.

Coriander leaves: also known as fresh dhana leaves. It is an invigorating herb derived from the annual plant *Coriandrum sativam* grown and used extensively in warm climates worldwide. It is known to be the world's most widely used herb. Regularly used in Indian cuisine to garnish vegetable dishes, dals, savouries, and also used to make green chutneys.

Cumin seeds: Also known as jeera and sometimes known as safed jeera. Cumin is the dried seed of the herb *Cuminum cyminum*. The cumin plant grows to 30–50 cm tall and is harvested by hand. It is an herbaceous annual plant, with a slender branched stem 20–30 cm tall. The leaves are 5–10 cm long, pinnate or bipinnate, thread-like leaflets. Cumin seeds resemble caraway seeds, being oblong in shape, longitudinally ridged and yellow-brown in colour, like other members of the umbelliferae family such as caraway, parsley and dill. The flavour and aroma emerges most after they have been dried or added to hot ghee.

Curry leaves: known as *Murraya koenigii,* an aromatic leaf often used in Indian cuisine. The leaf is derived from a small tree, growing 4-6 m tall, with a trunk up to 40 cm diameter. The leaves are pinnate, with 11-21 leaflets, each leaflet 2-4 cm long and 1-2 cm broad. The leaves are also used as a herb in Ayurvedic medicine and also contain iron.

Dal / Dhal: in India any type of dried bean, pea or lentil is called dal. These husked and split lentils are used to make savouries and soups as they are easy to cook, easy to digest and provides a valuable source of protein in the vegetarian diet.

Darsana: audience with a revered personality or a Deity.

Dasa: meaning servant (masculine). An appellation which along with a name of Krishna or one of His devotee given to a devotee at the time of initiation.

Deity: a God or Goddess, the state of being divine.

Devi Dasi: meaning servant (feminine).

Dhana jeera: Mixture of roasted and ground coriander and cumin seeds. Ratio of 4:1 to 2:1 of coriander:cumin.

Dudhi or Doodhi: is also known as bottle gourd, milk gourd or white pumpkin in English and Lauki in Hindi.

Dokra: spongy spicy fermented wheat cake.

Drumsticks: The drumstick tree or horseradish tree is one of the commonest trees in India. It is distributed in the wild in the sub-Himalayan tract and cultivated widely throughout India. The green skinned tough, 36 cm long, stick like vegetable, is surprisingly soft and fleshy inside. The opaque white flesh, embedded with pea-like seeds, covered in layers of skins, is sweetish, fragrant and tasty to eat, when cooked. They get their name from the fact that they do resemble the musical drumsticks.

Ekadasi: the eleventh day of both the waxing and waning moon. On Ekadasi devotees simplify their diet by abstaining from grains, beans and peas and increase their remembrance of Krishna by intensifying their chanting of the Hare Krishna mantra and other devotional activities.

ENO: is the most global of GlaxoSmithKline's (GSK) gastrointestinal products. The fast-acting effervescent fruit salts, used as an antacid and reliever of bloatedness, was invented in the 1850s by James Crossley Eno (1827-1915). It has sales of nearly £30 million, with its major markets being Spain, India, Brazil, South Africa, Malaysia and Thailand. It is frequently used as a substitute for baking powder. Each 5 gram of ENO contains sodium bicarbonate 2.32 g, *citric acid* 2.18 g and anhydrous sodium carbonate 0.50 g.

Fenugreek: Known as methi this is a small legume. The cuboid yellow to amber coloured fenugreek seeds are frequently used in the preparation of pickles, curry powders, and curry paste and the spice is often encountered in the *cuisine* of the Indian subcontinent. The plant is native to western Asia and south eastern Europe. Fenugreek leaves are also popular and are widely used in vegetable dishes, breads and savouries. The seeds have a bitter taste.

Garam masala: a mixture of dry-roasted spices well used in Indian cuisine. The word garam literally means hot and refers to intensity of the spices. Garam masala is pungent but not hot. The composition of garam masala differs regionally. A typical version of garam masala is peppercorn, cloves, cumin seeds, cardamon, nutmeg, star anise, coriander seeds and cinnamon. Unless otherwise specified garam masala is usually added toward the end of the cooking a concluding garnish of flavour like paprika or seasoned pepper.

Ghee: clarified butter. Its delicate flavour and special qualities make it the best of all cooking mediums. Ghee can be obtained from most supermarkets, oriental and Indian shops. However to prepare ghee, the butter is usually melted in a stainless steel vessel over medium high heat. The butter begins to melt, forming a white froth on top. It is then simmered, stirring occasionally and the froth begins to thin slowly and the colour of butter changes to a pale yellow shade. Then it is cooked on low heat until it turns a golden colour. The residue solids settle at the bottom and the ghee, which is now clear, golden and translucent with a fragrant smell, is ready. The ghee is then filtered through a muslin cloth, and it will solidify when completely cool. Ghee can be stored for extended periods without refrigeration, provided that it is kept in an airtight container to prevent oxidation and remains moisture free. The texture, colour or taste of ghee depends on the source of the milk from which the butter was made and the extent of boiling and simmering. Ghee is ideal for deep-frying because its smoke point is 250°C which is well above typical cooking temperatures of around 200°C and above that of most vegetable oils. Ayurveda considers ghee to be sattvik (in the mode of goodness) when used in cooking.

Ginger root: is the rhizome of the plant *Zingiber officinale*, consumed as a delicacy, medicine or spice. It lends its name to its genus and family (Zingiberaceae). Other notable members of this plant family are turmeric, cardamom and galangal. Ginger cultivation began in South Asia and has since spread to East Africa and the Caribbean. It is sometimes called ginger root to distinguish it from other things that share the name *ginger*. Fresh ginger is one of the main spices used for making lentil curries, vegetable preparations and savouries. In western cuisines ginger is traditionally used mainly in sweet foods eg biscuits, breads, cakes and drinks.

Gokul: The most celebrated of Shree Krishna's abodes.

Goshala milk: is milk obtained from cows living in the Bhaktivedanta goshalas, which is a protective shelter for their cows. Goshalas focus on treating cows in accordance with Hinduism philosophy. The cows and bulls live peacefully the full duration of their lives. Bulls are trained to work at an early age and assist in agricultural production by ploughing fields and pulling carts. The calves drink milk from their mothers till they reach the age of seven to ten months to ensure good health. The cows are always milked by hand.

Gulab jamun: a sweet made out of deep-fried powdered milk balls, soaked in flavoured sweet.

Guvar: also known as cluster beans.

Halva (Halava): a dessert made from toasted coarse semolina, butter and sugar.

Hare Krishna mantra: the great mantra Hare Krishna Hare Krishna Krishna Krishna Hare Hare Hare Rama Hare Rama Rama Rama Hare Hare. Hare is the personal form of God's own happiness, His eternal consort, Srimati Radharani. Krishna "the all-attractive one," and Rama," the all pleasing one" are the names of God. This prayer means "My dear Radharani and Krishna please engage me in Your devotional service." The *Vedas* recommend the chanting of the Hare Krishna mantra as the easiest and most sublime way of awakening one's dormant love of God.

Idli: is a savoury cake of South Indian origin, popular throughout India. The cakes are usually 5 cm in diameter and are made by steaming a batter consisting urad dal and rice. The fermentation process breaks down the starches so that they are more readily metabolized by the body.

ISKCON: The International Society for Krishna Consciousness. (The Hare Krishna movement).

Jagannatha: is a deity worshiped primarily by Hindu people, mainly in the Indian state of Orissa. Jagannatha is considered a form of Vishnu and Lord Jagannatha is worshipped as part of a triad "Ratnabedi" along with his brother Balabhadra deva and sister devi Subhadra. The oldest and most famous Jagannatha deity is established in Puri, in Orissa. The temple of Jagannatha in Puri is regarded as one of the Char Dhama. Lord Jagannatha's favourite sweet is called Jagannatha tongues.

Jaggery: (also transliterated as *jaggeree*) is a traditional unrefined, non-centrifugal, whole cane sugar consumed in Asia, Africa, Latin America and the Caribbean. It is a concentrated product of cane juice without separation of the molasses and crystals, and can vary from golden brown to dark brown in colour. It contains up to 50 % sucrose, up to 20 % inverted sugars, moisture content of up to 20 % and the remainder made up of other insoluble matter such as wood ash, proteins and bagasse fibers. Jaggery is used as an ingredient in both sweet and savory dishes across India and Sri Lanka.

Kachori: or kachauri or katchuri is a spicy snack popular in various parts of India including Uttar Pradesh, Rajasthan, Delhi, Maharashtra, Madhya Pradesh, Gujarat, Bengal and Orissa. It is usually a round flattened ball made of fine flour filled with a stuffing like peas or dals and which is a delicacy in Bengal.

Kadee: It is a spicy dish whose thick gravy is based on gram flour / chickpea flour (called Besan in Hindi) and to which yogurt is added to give it a little sour taste. It is often eaten with boiled rice or chapati.

Kalonji seeds: *Nigella sativa* is an annual flowering plant, native to south and southwest Asia. It grows to 20–30 cm tall, with finely divided, linear (but not thread-like) leaves. The flowers are delicate and usually coloured pale blue and white, with five to ten petals. The fruit is a large and inflated capsule composed of three to seven united follicles, each containing numerous seeds. The seed is used as a spice. For some reason they are called black cumin seeds or onion seeds, (but not related to the onion). They are small black and tear dropped shaped. Kalonji seeds have a peppery and herbal taste. They are used as part of the spice mixture punch pooran (five spices) and by itself used in great many Bengali cuisine recipes.

Karela: a bitter gourd valued in Vedic cuisine for its beneficial effects on the digestive system.

Karhai / Karai: a bowl-shaped pan similar to the Chinese wok, with high sloping walls and a rounded bottom. It is usually made of thick iron and can vary in size from (30-35 cm) for home use or 3-4 feet (1 metre) for restaurant use. There are handles on both sides and the karhai is mainly used for deep-frying or pan-frying.

Kathmir vada: a spicy savoury made from chickpea, water and yogurt, seasoned, and cooked. It is then allowed to set, cut into diamond shapes and fried. The ingredients used are identical to khandvi the presentation is different.

Khandvi: is a popular snack amongst Gujaratis, especially amongst the children. Nobody can hide their love for this delicious savoury made of chickpea flour and yogurt, tempered with mustard and sesame seeds. At the same time, none can deny that it is a difficult item to prepare. Be patient, and remember to cook the paste slowly and completely till thick. Also, take care to roll the khandvi lightly and temper well.

Khoa: When milk is boiled down until much of the water (85 % by weight) is evaporated, the soild, dough-like mass (about one-sixth of the total volume) that remains when mixed with suger it is called *khoa*.

Krishna: the Supreme Personality of Godhead meaning infinitely attractive.

Lassi: is a popular and traditional yogurt-based drink of the Indian subcontinent. It is made by blending yogurt with water and Indian spices. Traditional lassi (also known as salted lassi or, simply lassi) is a savory drink sometimes flavored with ground roasted cumin and black salt, while sweet lassi on the other hand, is blended with sugar or fruits instead of spices.

Lauki: also known as dudhi or doodhi or bottle gourd, milk gourd or white pumpkin in English.

Linseed (brown flaxseed): can be bought from and Health Food Store and they come in two basic varieties brown and yellow or golden. Linseeds are powerhouses of nutrition. Most types have similar nutritional charateristics and equal numbers of short-chain omega-3 fatty acids. They have a subtle nutty, slightly earthy flavour and a cheap superfood that everyone can include in their diet. Linseeds may lower cholesterol levels, and is a natural remedy for IBS and constipation.

Maha: means great.

Malpura: sweet dumplings in flavoured yogurt.

Masala: a blend of spices.

Matoki: or green cooking bananas or plantain have its origins from the tropical parts of Asia and Africa. There are many varieties of cooking bananas. The Matoki variety comes from Uganda. Matoki are starchy vegetables. Unlike a ripe banana, Matoki are less sweet and need to be cooked before they can be eaten.

Meringue: is a crisp, cooked mixture of sugar and egg-whites. In our recipe we have substituted the egg-white with linseeds which in themselves are very healthy. Linseeds when cooked resemble egg-whites in their consistency and propensities.

Methi: also known as fenugreek has three culinary uses as a herb (dried or fresh leaves), as a spice (seeds) and as a vegetable (fresh leaves, sprouts, and microgreens).

Mustard seeds: or black rai are the small round seeds of various mustard plants. The seeds are usually about 1 or 2 mm in diameter. Mustard seeds may be coloured from yellowish white to black. They are important spices in many regional foods. The seeds can come from three different plants: black mustard (*Brassica nigra*), brown Indian mustard (*B. juncea*) and white mustard (*Bhirta/Sinapis alba*). In Indian cuisine the seeds are fried in hot ghee to extract nutty and pungent flavour before adding to vegetables, chutneys and raitas. In Bengali cooking mustard seeds is one of the ingredients for punch pooram (5 spices).

Ondwa: flour obtained from Indian grocery shops is a mixture of gram flour or finely ground channa dal, rice and turmeric powder.

Okra / Bhindi: known in many English-speaking countries as lady's fingers or gumbo, is a flowering plant in the mallow family. It is valued for its edible green seed pods. The geographical origin of okra is disputed, with supporters of South Asian, Ethiopian and West African origins. The plant is cultivated in tropical, subtropical and warm temperate regions around the world.

Pakora: is a fried snack (fritter) found across South Asia. The word *pakora* is derived from Sanskrit *pakvavata*, a compound of *pakva* 'cooked' and *vata* 'a small lump' or its derivative *vataka* 'a round cake made of pulse fried in ghee'. Pakoras are created by taking one or two ingredients such potato, spinach, plantain, cauliflower, tomato, chilli or occasionally bread and dipping them in a batter of gram flour and then deep-frying them.

Paneer: freshly prepared cheese made from hot milk and a curdling agent such as lemon juice, yogurt, citric acid or whey. There is no need for using rennet as the coagulation agent, thus making it completely vegetarian and providing one of the sources of protein. Common paneer dishes are sandesh, rasagulla, rasamalai, mutter paneer, saag paneer, paneer tikka, pakora and chilli paneer.

Paratha: is an Indian flat-bread that originated in the Indian subcontinent. *Paratha* is an amalgamation of the words *parat* and *atta* which literally means layers of cooked dough. The paratha can be round, heptagonal, square or triangular and is made by pan frying whole-wheat dough on a tava.

Parwar: *richosanthes dioica* is also known as the pointed gourd or parwal or parval (from Hindi) or potol. Colloquially, in India, it is often called *green potato*. It is widely cultivated in the eastern part of India, particularly in Orissa, Bengal, Assam, Bihar and Uttar Pradesh. It is a good source of carbohydrates, vitamin A and vitamin C. It also contains major nutrients and trace elements (magnesium, potassium, copper, sulfur, and chlorine) which are needed in small quantities, for playing essential roles in human physiology.

Patra: is a popular vegetarian dish in the West region of India. It is known as Patra in Gujarat and

Patrode in the Konkan region of India. Its main ingredient is crushed chickpeas (gram flour), wrapped in the leaf of the Taro plant (*Colocasia esculenta*). Many different ways exist to prepare the dish it is commonly rolled up with spices and tamarind paste, then sliced and fried. It is possible to buy tins of prepared rolls of patra. Fresh patra leaves can be purchased from Indian grocery shops.

Pera: is a milk sweet which is a mixture of khoa and sugar when heated over a low flame.

Prasadam or **prasada:** remnants of food and other items offered to the Supreme Lord. By accepting Krishna Prasada one can rapidly become purified and achieves the love of Godhead.

Pudla: a delicious chickpea savoury pancake.

Pujari: a pujari is a temple priest and have a reputation for being learned. They also conduct prayer services.

Punch pooran: also known as Panch Puran, Panchphoran, Panch Phutana (Oriya) or Five-spice Mix is a spice blend used in Bangladesh and Eastern India, especially in Bengali, Assamese and Oriya cuisine. In Assamese and Bengali, panch phoran and in Oriya, panch phutana, literally mean "Five Spices". (This spice mix is of Bengali origin also known as Punch Pooran). Equal quantities of whole spices are simply mixed together without roasting or grinding. The five spices include: cumin seeds, fennel seeds, fenugreek seeds, mustard seeds and kalonji seeds.

Puri: a small deep-fried flat bread made from white flour, whole-wheat flour or a mixture of both.

Raita: made with yogurt and used as a sauce, dip or salad. The yogurt is mixed with grated, raw vegetables eg cucumber and carrot and seasoned. The origin of the word *Raita* is dated around 19th century and it comes from Hindi language. The word *Raita* in Hindi and Urdu is a derivative of the Sanskrit word *Rajika* meaning black mustard and *tiktaka* meaning sharp or pungent.

Rasagulla: is a very popular cheese-based spongy syrupy sweet dish originally from the Indian states of West Bengal and Orissa. It is popular throughout India and other parts of South Asia. The dish is made from balls of paneer (an Indian cottage cheese) and semolina dough, cooked in light syrup made of sugar until the sugar enters the balls.

Rose water: also known as rose syrup is the diluted essence of rose petals. It is widely used throughout the Middle East as a flavouring agent. In India it is used mainly in sweets.

Saffron: or *kesar* is the hand picked stigmas called threads collected from the flowers the saffron crocus (*Crocus sativus*) cultivated in the Mediterranean, Asia Minor, India and China. Today most cooks agree the best saffron is obtained from Spain. Saffron has a pleasantly spicy, pungent, slightly bitter honey-like taste with a strong potent colouring power. The saffron threads should be soaked in water or milk and ground or slightly dry-roasted and powdered before use. This helps release the beneficial components. Worth noting saffron is an expensive spice and to use sparingly.

Samo seeds: looks somewhere between coarse semolina and couscous. Samo rice is one of the foods eaten during fast days such as Ekadasi.

Samosa: a vegetable or paneer filled triangular crusted savoury pastries.

Sandesh: is a famous Indian milk sweet made from fresh paneer with sugar.

Sannyasa: the renounced order of life for spiritual culture, the fourth order of life (ashrama). Free from family relationships and with all activities dedicated to pleasing Krishna.

Sukta: a traditional Bengali bitter dish made up of a mixture of five different vegetables cooked and spiced with punch pooran. The taste is bitter and is best served at lunch time to help digestion.

Tamarind: also know as Imli (*Tamarindus indica*) is a tree in the family Fabaceae indigenous to tropical Africa. The genus *Tamarindus* is a monotypic taxon, having only a single species. The tamarind tree produces edible, pod-like fruit which are extensively used in various cuisines around the world. The pulp is extracted from the brown pods. Fresh pulp has a sour fruity taste which is extensively used in Indian cooking. Native to Sudan, Cameroon, Nigeria and Oman. The most convenient form is available as a concentrate. Tamarind makes excellent sweet and sour chutneys or sauces and can also be used in vegetable dishes.

Tava: flat iron, hot plate used for cooking flatbreads like chapatis and parathas.

Tindora: *Coccinia grandis*, the ivy gourd also known as baby watermelon, little gourd or gentleman's toes is a tropical vine. Indian Ivy Gourd is a widely consumed vegetable, available in India through out the year. Called Dondakaya (Telugu) or Tindora / Tondli (Hindi), these cute looking small, stubby, green colored vegetables which grow aggressively on vines are used to prepare delicious stuffed curries, stews, pickles, salads and stir fries.

Toovar: also known as arhar dal, tuvar dal or yellow spilt peas. It is this split dal widely used for Gujarati dals, puran poli and lots of other tasty variety of dish. Toor dal / dahl is the most popular lentil in India they are also called Thuvaram paruppu or kandhi pappu. Toovar dal exhibits a thick gelatinous consistency. They take a little longer to cook than moong or masoor dal / dahl.

Toria: The ridge gourd is an extremely popular vegetable in Africa, Asian and Arabic countries. It is also known by other names as loofah, luffa turai, turiya tori etc. It is dark green ridged vegetable having white seeds embedded in spongy flesh.

Tulasi: sacred plant most dear to Lord Krishna which belongs to the basil family.

Turmeric: (*Curcuma longa*) is a rhizomatous, herbaceous, perennial plant of the ginger family, Zingiberaceae. It is native to tropical South Asia and needs temperatures between 20°C and 30°C and a considerable amount of annual rainfall to thrive. Plants are gathered annually for their rhizomes, and propagated from some of those rhizomes in the following season.When not used fresh, the rhizomes are boiled for several hours and then dried in hot ovens, after which they are ground into a deep orange-yellow powder. It is commonly used as a spice in curries and other South Asian and Middle Eastern cuisine, for dyeing and to impart color to mustard condiments. Its active ingredient is curcumin and it has a distinctly earthy, slightly bitter, slightly hot peppery flavour. Ancient Indian medicine has recommended its use in food for its medicinal value.

Vaisnava: is a devotee of Lord Visnu an expansion of Krishna.

Vanilla: is a flavouring derived from orchids of the genus *Vanilla*, primarily from the Mexican species, Flat-leaved Vanilla (*V. planifolia*). The word *vanilla* derives from the Spanish word "vainilla", *little pod*. Pre-Columbian Mesoamerican peoples cultivated vanilla and Spanish conquistador Hernán Cortés is credited with introducing both vanilla and chocolate to Europe in the 1520s. Vanilla is the second most expensive spice after saffron, because growing the vanilla seed pods is labor-intensive. Despite the expense, vanilla is highly valued for its flavour, which author Frederic Rosengarten, Jr. described in *The Book of Spices* as "pure, spicy and delicate."

Valor: is a type of broad bean which is bitter in taste and best prepared with other vegetables like potatoes, peas and aubergines. The preparation is similar to shelling peas. Remove the out stringer thread down the bean, split the bean in to two and cut the bean into smaller pieces.

Whey: Whey is a co-product of paneer production. It is one of the components that separates from milk after curdling, with lemon juice, yogurt or citric acid.

ABOUT HIS DIVINE GRACE
A.C. BHAKTIVEDANTA SWAMI SRILA PRABHUPADA

1896: 1st September His Divine Grace A.C. Bhaktivedanta Swami Srila Prabhupada was born in Kolkata, India as Abhay Charan De.

1922: Srila Prabhupada met his spiritual master Srila Bhaktisiddanta Saraswati Goswami, a prominent religious scholar and the founder of the 64 Gaudiya Matha. In that first meeting Srila Prabhupada was given his first instruction by his spiritual master. The comment of dedicating his life to teaching Vedic knowledge particularly in English would change his life and the world.

1933: Srila Prabhupada took initiation from Srila Bhaktisiddhanta Saraswati Goswami at Allahabad.

1944: Srila Prabhupada started the ("Back to Godhead" an English fortnightly magazine) single handed.

1950: Srila Prabhupada retired from married life and adopted the Vanaprastha (retired) order of life. He lived in the historic temple of Radha-Damodar in Vrindaban.

1959: Srila Prabhupada took sannyasa and started a multi volume commentated translation of the 18,000 verse of the Srimad Bhagavatam.

1965: Having published three volumes of the Srimad Bhagavatam, Srila Prabhupada boarded a cargo ship called the Jaladuta from Kolkata and set sail for Boston Harbour in USA, to fulfill the mission of his spiritual master.

1966: In July after almost a full year of difficulty and practically penniless Srila Prabhupada established The International Society for Krishna Consciousness (ISKCON) in New York.

1973: 21st August Srila Prabhupada installed the deities Sri Sri Radha-Gokulananda at Bhaktivedanta Manor, Watford, UK.

1977: 14 th November Srila Prabhupada passed away in Vrindaban, India. In his last 12 years Srila Prabhupada guided the society and seen it grow to a worldwide confederation of more than 100 ashrams, schools, temple institutions and farm communities. Srila Prabhupada's most significant contribution were his books. Srila Prabhupada circled the globe 14 times on lecture tours that took him to 6 continents.

OFFERING FOOD TO KRISHNA

Cooking for Krishna is a pleasure. After cooking place all the cooked foods, drinks, fruits, savouries, chutneys, rice, breads, drinks and sweets, plus water on plates solely for offering to Krishna and place the items on a table.

If you are new to offering your food to Krishna then the easiest method would be the recitation of the maha mantra.

hare krishna hare krishna krishna krishna hare hare
hare rama hare rama rama rama hare hare

However you can recite the prayers the devotees use.

In front of the altar sit on a mat kept only for worshipping purposes and while ringing a bell recite three times the pranama prayers to your spiritual master begging permission to assist him in his service to the Lord.

The following pranama prayers can also be recited to Srila Prabhupada if you have not been initiated. Repeat each verse three times.

nama om visnu-padaya krishna-prethaya bhu-tale
srimate bhaktivedante-svamin iti namine

I offer my respectful obeisances unto His Divine Grace A.C. Bhaktivedanta Swami Prabhupada, who is very dear to Lord Krishna having taken shelter at His lotus feet.

namas te sarasvate deve gaura-vani pracarine
nirvisesa sunyavadi pascatya-dsea-tarine

Our respectful obeisances are onto you, O spiritual master, servant of Sarasvati Gosvami. You are kindly preaching the message of Lord Caitanya and delivering the Western countries which are filled with impersonalism and voidism.

Now chant the following prayer to Lord Caitanya requesting His mercy:

namo maha-vadanyaya krishna-prema-pradaya te
krishnaya krishna-chaitanya-namne gaura-tvise namah

O most munificent incarnation! You are Krishna Himself appearing as Sri Krishna Caitanya Mahaprabhu. You have assumed the golden colour of Srimati Radharani and You are widely distributing pure love of Krishna. We offer our respectful obesiances unto You.

Now chant the following prayer offering respects to Lord Krishna:

namo brahmanya-devaya go-brahmana-hitaya ca
jagad-dhitaya krishnaya govindaya namo namah

Let me offer my respectful obeisances unto Lord Krishna, who is the worshipable Deity for all brahminical men, who is the well-wisher of cows and the brahmanas and who is always benefitting the whole world. I offer my repeated obeisances to the Personality of Godhead known as Krishna and Govinda.

jaya sri-krishna-caitanya prabhu nityananda
sri-advaita gadadhara srivasadi-gaura-bhakta vrnda

All glories to Sri Caitanya Mahaprabhu accompanied by His eternal associates Sri Nityananda Prabhu. Sri Advaita Prabhu, Sri Gadadhara Prabhu and all His devotees headed by Srivasa Prabhu.

hare kirshna hare krishna krishna krishna hare hare
hare rama hare rama rama rama hare hare

My dear Lord Krishna, my dear Lord Rama, O energy of the Lord, Hara please engage me in Your service.

After offering the food to the Lord wait for 5-10 minutes depending on the size of the offering, for Raja Bhoga we wait for 25 minutes for Lord Krishna to partake of the preparations.

At the end of the time clap your hands three times ring a bell and remove the plates praying that you have served the Lord and His associates to Their full Satisfaction.

Then transfer the prasadam from the Lords plates to other containers for serving.

About Mother Kulangana Devi Dasi

Mother Kulangana was born in Warsaw, Poland on 3rd May 1932. She joined ISKCON at Bury Place, London 1972 and took initiation from Srila Prabhupada in 1974.

Mother Kulangana moved to The Hare Krishna Temple, New Vrindaban, USA in 1978. For three years Bhaktin Nidi taught her how to make sandesh for the Deities and she learned how to make burfi and pera from Dharmakala Devi Dasi.

The skill Mother Kulangana acquired from New Vrindaban for making mangala arati sweets is perfected and has been passed down to other devotees.

Mother Kulangana lives at Bhaktivedanta Manor and still enjoys making mangala arati sweets.

About The Author

Dhama Sevana Dasa was born in Poland in 1973 named Dominik Dyjecinski. He met the Hare Krishna devotees in 1989 and became a full time devotee with ISKCON in 1992.

After living with the devotees in the Warsaw temple for nearly two years he moved to London in 1994 and was initiated by His Grace Krishna Kshetra Prabhu in 1995 and continued to live at Bhaktivedanta Manor for four years.

He is married to Gopa Kishori Devi Dasi, has two children and now lives near Bhaktivedanta Manor.

If you would like to correspond with him about the subject matter of this book please write to:

info@rajabhoga.com

Bibliography

1). The Hare Krishna Book of Vegetarian Cooking. Adiraja Dasa

2). The Art of Indian Vegetarian Cooking. Yamuna Devi

3). A Handbook of Vaisnava Songs and Practices Complied and edited by Ramanujacharya Dasa

4). The Hare Krishna Music Book. Complied and arranged by Joan Wilder

INDEX

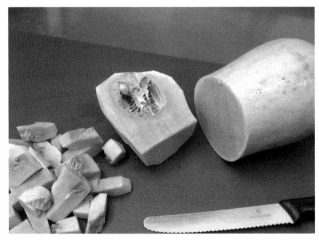

Butternut squash page 60, 84 and 94 for pumpkin replacement

Cassava / Mogo page 279

Chillies / Ginger used in almost all the recipes

Coriander leaves used for garnishing and chutneys

Curry leaves page 22, 28 and 38

Drumsticks page 60, 74, 94

Eggplant, baby (aubergines) page 90

Green cooking bananas (matoki)
page 60, 72

Guvar page 106

Karela page 76, 78, 80, 82

Lauki (dudhi) page 52, 54, 56

Methi page 98, 106

Okra page 86, 88

Parwar (potols) page 96

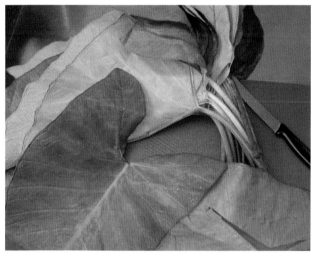

Patra leaves page 147

Tindora page 100

Toria page 50

Valor page 104

Chana Dal page 32

Mung dal page 28

Toovar dal page 34

Urad dal used in many savouries
page 156,158

Yellow split mung dal page 30

Flavourings

Vanilla pods and essence page 240

Linseed (flaxseed) page 228

Ajwain seeds used in valor, guvar recipes. Good for digestion

Aniseed used for flavouring sweet rice

Asafetida used in almost all recipes as a substitute for onion

Bay leaves varied usage ie flavour sweet rice or add to dals, chutneys

Black salt used mainly for salads some chutneys and roasted nuts

Cardamon powder for flavouring milk, shrikand, pera and burfi

Chilli powder limited use in chutneys and savoury dishes

Cinnamon sticks can used in almost all preparations, adds flavour

Cinnamon powder good for baking and fillings for savouries

Cloves (whole), add to dals, rice and fruit chutneys

Cumin seeds extensively used

Dhana jeera powder used in many of our recipes

Dry mango powder a lemon juice substitute for some dals and okra

Dry methi leaves excellent for puris and pakoras

Fenugreek (whole) seeds added when cooking spinach and dals

Fennel seeds a sweet spice can be added to hot drinks

Garam masala used in some of our dishes and in savoury fillings

Ground cloves for savoury fillings, alupatra, kachoris

Ground ginger for baking cakes or cookies

Ground pepper/pepper used in salads savouries and some dishes

Kalonji seeds mainly added to puries, pakoras and samosa pastry

Mixed herbs (whole) for salad dressing and ratatouille

Mixed spice used in baking

Mustard seeds used in almost all our dishes and savoury toppings

Nutmeg a sweet spice added to hot milk, halva and used in baking

Panch pooran a blend of 5 spices used in many Bengali dishes/sukta

Paprika powder a popular spice for salads and savoury dishes

Turmeric powder used in almost all our recipes rice, dals, savouries

White poppy seeds used to Indian sweets or some Bengali dishes

Whole cardamons to flavour sweet syrups, hot milk or sweet rice

Whole red chillies used in chutneys and some dals and dishes

Whole dhania seeds used in dals and some of our dishes

Whole spices in a container providing easy access while cooking

Groumd spices in a container providing easy access while cooking

Jananivas Prabhu

Head pujari of Mayapura Chandrodaya Mandir, West Bengal, India accepts the Raja Bhoga recipe cookbook with appreciation

"The cookbook you gave me is great. I use it every time I cook. Easy to follow and ideal for Pujari cooking. Thank you".

- Murli Manohara Dasa Head Pujari, Radha-Londonisvara, Hare Krishna Temple, Soho, London.

"Thanks for the files. Certainly looks like a wonderful book full of devotion and tender loving care for its production".

- Advaita Candra Dasa, Torchlight publishers, Mayapur, India.

"Just a few minutes ago, on this most auspicious day of Sri Krishna Janmastami, I received the beautiful Raja Bhoga Recipes at my doorstep. I have only looked through a few pages quickly and it is so nicely designed and easy on the eyes, thanks to the large print and having the photo and ingredients on one side; instructions on the other. It lays flat and can be placed under an acrylic cookbook holder so it stays clean while cooking".

- Kalindi Devi Dasi

"Congratulations Kishor. Awesome achievement".

- Dr Vijay Nathoo

"Just thought of you as I cooked a proper big meal for my deities from your book. I'm so touched by the book it is amazing. Deities are just munching away so will tell you how it tastes once they have eaten and I have honoured their reminance".

- Anonymous

"Haribol just to let u know i used your recipe book and made lemon curd tart for Their Lordships Sri Sri Radha-Gokulananda, the tart came out really nice & tasty. I followed the instructions as in the book. Few other people tried it and glorified it too".

- Ragatmika Radhika Devi Dasi

"For the past 20 years I have been in the food industry working in hotels / restaurants with a keen interest in preparing and sampling food. I am currently employed in corporate managament.

During the 20 years I scoured through hundreds of recipe books and recently I was given this Raja Bhoga recipe book which surpasses all the others. My wife and I tried at least 7 recipes and all turned out exactly as described in this well written easy to follow cookbook. I stongly recommend this book to you".

- Ashutosh Bhardwaj (BA, Degree in Hotel Management, Masters Certificate in Strategic Hospitality Management Cornell University, New York).

"I haven't looked at it in detail. I have flicked through it. Very interesting traditional and fussion recipes. Easy to read and yummy and delicious photos, just looking at the photos one would want to use the recipes. Will give you more feedback once I have made a few. Also love the introduction linking meditation to food".

- Hema

"It is very easy to see that a great deal of time and care has gone into the meticulously detailed recipes compiled. I am so glad I bought this book and made apple pie and what great success!!!! Thank you so much Dhama Sevana".

- Anupama Radhika Devi Dasi

"This is the best cookbook I have seen in a longtime. Having tested virtually all the preps on offer I am so happy to now have the chance to make them too. With easy instructions and a pragmatic approach I can't wait to use it next time we travel. Dhama Sevana and Krishna Kishor have done amazingly well".

- Ben den Ouden, Wellington, New Zealand.

"Haribol Dhama, I really appreciate your service and dedication on this cookbook, as well as Krishna Kishor prabhu. I think it is the best cookbook in ISKCON at the moment. I am not saying that because you are my friend but because I really think that way".

- Niti Laksha Dasa

"It gives me great pleasure to commend both Krishna Kishor Prabhu and Dhama Sevana Prabhu for sharing their secrets and making available to the entire world an easy to follow guide to vegetarian cooking. The real taste is present in every recipe. Is it devotion / love or both?".

- Svayam Jyoti Krishna Dasa

"Hare Krishna Dhama Sevana and Krishna Kishor Prabhus. Both of us are novice cooks. We have used your Raja Bhoga recipe book whilst we have had the opportunity to cook for their Lordships in Radharani's Kitchen at the Manor.

I had never ever thought that we would be able to make Halva / Sabji / Fruit Chutney....but having followed the step by step guidance in the book, we managed it.

My wife also managed to cook kachories all on her own. It is a very well written book and I am glad you have started to update it.

Good Luck and Thank You".

- Damodar Krishna Dasa (Durgesh Desai B.Com F.C.C.A) and Rasika Lila Devi Dasi

"Love Dhama Sevana's recipes - they are simple proven to work and preps taste great especially our favourite Tomato peas and paneer".

- Malini Nitai Devi Dasi